WOMAN
BE FREE!

WOMAN BE FREE!

PATRICIA GUNDRY

ZONDERVAN
PUBLISHING HOUSE

OF THE ZONDERVAN CORPORATION | GRAND RAPIDS, MICHIGAN 49506

Unless otherwise indicated, Scripture quotations are taken from
The New American Standard Bible, © 1960, 1972 by
The Lockman Foundation. Used by permission.

WOMAN, BE FREE
© 1977 by The Zondervan Corporation
Grand Rapids, Michigan

This edition   1979

Library of Congress Cataloging in Publication Data
Gundry, Patricia
   Woman, be free.

    1.   Woman (Theology)—Biblical teaching.
2.   Women in church work.   I.   Title.
BS680.W7G86   262.8'34'12   76-30494

ISBN 0-310-25361-6

Printed in the United States of America

Contents

You shall know the truth,
and the truth shall make
you free (John 8:32).

1

The Problem: Second-Class Christians

1

The Problem: Second-Class Christians

> It is strange that Paul's total picture of woman's participation in the life of the church has been so completely overlooked in an uncritical acceptance of two of his isolated statements. Through this kind of selective obedience to the Scriptures, a general theological position concerning male-female relationships in the church has been built upon particular directives that are in conflict with the pervasive biblical view on this matter. As a consequence, the role traditionally given to women in the church would seem to indicate an acceptance of society's view of woman rather than God's view.[1]

Many women in our churches feel like second-class Christians. The generic term *man* as used in the Bible repeatedly refers to mankind in general, but women are excluded from the application of many of these passages. It is as though an invisible hand rises to bar their way when they attempt to appropriate these passages for themselves.

There have always been women who questioned the validity of their restricted service in the church. However, the citing of a few selected Bible verses or an argument based on "logic" was usually sufficient to silence all but the most persistent. If the questioner was not convinced, at least she kept her doubts to herself from then on.

Today, more than ever before, women are verbalizing those

doubts. They want to know why they must always be subject to men and why they may not use the abilities and opportunities they feel God has given them. Many women are afraid to ask for these answers or to admit they doubt the validity of the rules they have been taught. Many become angry after discovering that the foundations for some of those rules are not as firm and changeless as they had assumed.

It is no wonder there are doubts. There are so many conflicting rules and regulations for women in our churches. Most of these regulations are supported by appeals to supposedly biblical principles or commandments and may consist of any one or more of the following:

A woman may not —
— pastor a church;
— speak in the morning worship service (although she may speak on Wednesday evening, or sing or present special music at any service, including the Sunday morning worship service);
— serve on any governing board in the church;
— serve in any capacity of authority in the church that involves a woman directing men;
— teach a class composed of both men and women, unless her husband is also present;
— teach a class with any men in it;
— speak at all in church;
— lead the congregation in singing unless it contains only females or children;
— direct a choir;
— wear cosmetics, short hair, short dresses, or pants.

A woman must —
— wear a hat in church;
— obey her husband or father unless his commands are unbiblical or immoral;
— obey her husband or father regardless of the command;
— believe that God directs her through her husband, making it unnecessary for God to deal with her directly;

— consider her husband's will for her life to be God's will for her life;

— not leave her husband regardless of the treatment she receives.

Women know that not all these practices can be right. They are asking for the opportunity to examine for themselves which rules *are* biblical.

But women have been silent for so long that the church tends not to take them seriously now when they ask to be heard. They have so often sat quietly in classes with men, rarely commenting on any subject, that many men believe women have nothing to contribute. This is not true. Women talk freely among themselves, but in mixed groups women somehow lose their confidence. They sense that their views are not considered to be of equal value with men's, so they remain quiet.

Women have been afraid that they truly are inferior persons. The statement that being inferior in position does not mean one is inferior in essence is not convincing. The analogies given as proof do not adequately substitute for facts. It seems to many women that either they actually are inferior and justly kept down, or they are treated unjustly by the church.

Perhaps part of the reason women are so restricted in our churches is that there has been almost no feminine perspective in either Bible translation or interpretation for over eighteen hundred years. Since women have been largely excluded from serious Bible study, teaching of Bible and theology in colleges and seminaries, translation from the original languages, and the pastorate, there is an almost total lack of female representation in Bible interpretation. Different people see different facets of truth. If the experiences of half of Christendom are not applicable to the careful study and translation of the Scriptures, then we are bound to miss a great deal and perhaps make mistakes a wider experience would prevent.

A rule of Bible interpretation quoted in every introductory hermeneutics class is, "If the first sense makes good sense, seek no other sense." Obviously a male interpreter, schooled in the traditional position of woman's inferior status, would have little trouble passing along that position without further study or comparison with other Scripture. His limited experience would not alert him to problems that a woman might see. To him, the first sense would be the traditional sense. Since it would be no problem to him, he would go on to other exegetical matters that seemed more important, not because he cared nothing for woman's plight, but because he was ignorant of it.

It matters a great deal whether women get a chance to interpret the Bible themselves. One man asked, "Couldn't the Holy Spirit reveal the woman's perspective to a man?" But why should He need to when there are plenty of women available?

Ask a black preacher if the subject of slavery in the Bible looked the same to a white churchman in the seventeenth or eighteenth century as it did to a slave. Most white churchmen firmly believed that slavery was biblical and just. They lacked the slave's perspective.

The result of our many restrictions and rules for women is an altered citizenship. *In practice,* women *are* second-class Christians. This second-class citizenship for women hurts us all. The church as a body is denied the internal freedom under which it flourishes best. It is denied the benefits from the spiritual and intellectual gifts of half its membership when those gifts conflict with its stereotyped views of the women possessing them. Every woman with something "unacceptable" to offer suffers, and those to whom she would minister lose her needed help.

Women who feel they must be inferior to their husbands are victims of our rigid role stereotypes, and their husbands are co-victims, for they consider themselves failures because they cannot fit into the scheme of always being superior to their wives.

Few churches exist where women hold positions as church officers (other than perhaps church clerk or secretary). Nor are women allowed to usher, collect the offering, lead the singing, make announcements, or offer public prayer. Are women incapable of such responsibilities? Certainly not.

It is as though the power structure in the church and ministry is labeled with a big sign: "For Men Only — God Says So!" But is that really what God said? When God moved Paul to write to the women of Corinth against speaking out in the meetings, was He telling women of all times that they could not open a meeting with prayer or give the announcements in their churches? Or was he trying to deal with a specific problem in the Corinthian church at that time? Women do not know.

It is time women looked at the Bible for themselves. It is time they examined the restrictions placed upon them and their supposed weaknesses that make them unfit for so much. What kind of creatures are they? What is their place in society and in the church? What does God think of them? What *can* they do?

We believe the Bible is God's message to His people. What does it really say about women?

Notes

[1]Lois Gunden Clemens, *Woman Liberated* (Scottsdale, PA: Herald Press, 1971), p. 137.

2

What Is Woman?

2

What Is Woman?

As I read, I became aware that there were two general types of observers; those who believed that pellagra was a man-made disease, the result of the inhuman practices of restricting the poor to a diet that cannot support health in a dog; and those who thought that it was the fault of the afflicted. The origins of these divergent opinions can repeatedly be traced to contemporary dissertations on the causes of poverty and malnutrition. As long as men have believed that human bondage is an inescapable partner of civilization and material progress, they have ascribed destitution to the inferior qualities of the destitute.[1]

WHAT WOMAN IS NOT

Woman has been treated as man's inferior in the church for so long that this practice has become accepted as truth. There is a continuing belief that woman is enigmatic, changeable, and non-understandable. Woman has been accused of being many things that she is not. And these myths have followed her from paganism into the church of the medieval age and persist to this day.

Woman is not inferior to man

From ancient days many men have considered woman to be an inferior creature. For example, Aristotle wrote that all females, both animal and human, were inferior to males.

17

> While still within the mother the female takes longer to develop than the male does; though once birth has taken place everything reaches its perfection sooner in females than in males — e.g., puberty, maturity, old age — because females are weaker and colder in their nature; and we should look upon the female state as being as it were a deformity, though one which occurs in the ordinary course of nature.[2]

Thomas Aquinas, whose influence on Western thought has been profound, was particularly admired for his "fearless reasoning and his ability to recognize and produce harmony and order." He echoed Aristotle's view of woman and made it the basis of her subjection to man.

> As regards the individual nature, woman is defective and misbegotten, for the active power in the male seed tends to the production of a perfect likeness according to the masculine sex; while the production of woman comes from defect in the active power, or from some material indisposition, or even from some external influence, such as that of a south wind, which is moist, as the Philosopher observes.
>
> Subjection is twofold. One is servile, by virtue of which a superior makes use of a subject for his own benefit; and this kind of subjection began after sin. There is another kind of subjection, which is called economic or civil, whereby the superior makes use of his subjects for their own benefit and good; and this kind of subjection existed even before sin. For the good of order would have been wanting in the human family if some were not governed by others wiser than themselves. So by such a kind of subjection woman is naturally subject to man, because in man the discernment of reason predominates.[3]

Freud, upon whose principles and ideas all of modern psychology has been based until recently, including "Christian" psychology, also held that women were inferior to men. He considered women's desires to accomplish something in their own right and determine their own actions to be abnormal and a result of envy of the male sex.

Were these men just woman-haters? No, they were thinkers wrestling with why things are as they are. But they approached the problem from only one viewpoint and worked backwards from the position: "If women have such an ignoble station in this world, there must be a reason. What is wrong with them that makes us treat them so badly?'' If women had been allowed to be philosophers, theologians, and psychologists, and if there had been a reversal of the treatment of men and women, we probably would have had the same type of reasoning concerning men. The fault is not in the philosophers, but in the narrowness of their viewpoint and experience.

There have been studies in recent years to determine if there *are* any differences between men and women aside from their sexual organs. There seem to be no specific differences that apply to all women or all men; but general differences appear in skeletal size, proportion of fatty tissue, and endurance levels. Men generally have larger muscles and more muscle strength, while women have more fatty tissue under the skin and greater endurance.

Differences in intelligence have not been proved. While there is some evidence to indicate that men *on the average* excel in certain intellectual fields and women *on the average* excel in others, it is impossible to determine if even this is influenced by cultural factors. We cannot devise a test to measure emotional differences between men and women; emotional and mental reactions are culturally conditioned at such an early age that there are no subjects available who are unaffected by this conditioning.

The Bible in its account of creation does not present woman as inferior to man. Both man and woman are created in God's image and both are given dominion over the earth. The later story of separate creation of male and female does not show a superiority-inferiority relationship but is a tender account of how God intended the sexes to relate to each other.

Much has been made of the words *helpmeet* and *helpmate*, as though they prove woman was a special added item created because the discovery was made that no other animal would do as helper to Adam. I think we are confused by our idea of what a helper means in our modern vocabulary. When we see the word *help*, we think of a subordinate, a domestic, or an apprentice, someone who is starting out at the bottom of the company ladder financially, socially, and influentially. We tend to think of Eve as

Adam's glorified girl Friday. But that is not at all the sense of the original language.

The words *help* and *meet* in the King James Version translate two Hebrew words, *ezer* and *neged*. The word *ezer* ("help") is never used in the Bible to refer to a subordinate helper but is used in reference to God as our Helper as in Psalm 121:1,2. The word *neged* is a preposition in Hebrew, but the most accurate way to translate it into English is by giving it a meaning such as "corresponding to" or "fit for" or "meet for." The idea is that Eve was an appropriate, fitting partner for Adam.

Jesus, our only human-divine glimpse of what God is really like, never treated women as inferiors. He went against the customs of His time and culture and shocked His disciples with His unconventional treatment of women. One just didn't speak to women in the manner of His conversation with the woman at the well. (To make it worse, a Samaritan woman was even a step further down the social ladder from other women.) Jesus encouraged Mary to listen to His teaching with the men rather than go to the kitchen where others thought she belonged. He accepted the woman taken in adultery as an equal to the men who were her accusers.

Woman is not the cause of the Fall

Woman has long been blamed and punished for eating that piece of fruit by being told she is not competent to make decisions or resist error because of that first mistake. That one who is mistreated or denied equality deserves bad treatment and a narrow life is an ancient excuse. It was present in paganism and soon infiltrated the early church. Tertullian, one of the early church further, had this to say about woman and the Fall:

> God's sentence hangs still over all your sex and His punishment weighs down upon you. You are the devil's gateway; you are she who first violated the forbidden tree and broke the law of God. It was you who coaxed your way around him whom the devil had not the force to attack. With what ease you shattered that image of God; man! Because of the death you merited, the Son of God had to die.[4]

These same accusations, in less forceful language, crop up in sermons and books today. They take many forms — everything from "Satan approached Eve because she was more emotional and thus more easily deceived" to "Adam willingly chose to sin in order not to be separated from her, but he wasn't deceived at all." The idea lingers that Eve was weak, whereas Adam was noble. The blame is placed on her.

There is one major flaw in all this punitive self-justification. The sin was disobedience. Adam and Eve both disobeyed. It does not matter which child takes the first cookie, nor does it matter how imaginative their excuses. Disobedience is disobedience. They both knew; they were created equal; they both sinned.

Woman is not a tempter of the pure

In the first century there was a restlessness in the Roman Empire. Many old religions were falling out of favor. People were searching for something more satisfying than the excesses and materialism of the Roman capital. Soldiers brought back stories of Eastern religions, and many new cults arose at this time. Gnostic beliefs were common among them, one of Gnosticism's basic beliefs being that the material world and the physical body were evil.

As Christianity spread, on its fringes were those who were adapting their view of Christianity to Gnosticism. It was believed by some that the way to know the truth was to separate oneself from physical needs and desires as much as possible. One could get used to old, drab clothes, not bathing, and eating sparingly, but sexual desires were persistent and hard to put off. For this reason sex was considered extremely evil. It was only a step further to declare the object of one's sexual desires evil.

The influence of Gnosticism spread until it was a serious threat to biblical Christianity by the middle of the second century. Even though it declined by the end of that century, it left its mark on the theology and practice of the developing church. Asceticism became not just a heretical fringe activity but a way for the pious to earn spiritual merit. Since by this time most of the preachers and church rulers were men, it is easy to understand why women came to be regarded more and more as tempters of the pure.

By the end of the second century women were considered dangerous by some of the church fathers. Clement of Alexandria wrote:

> Nothing disgraceful is proper for man, who is endowed with reason; much less for woman, to whom it brings shame even to reflect of what nature she is. . . . By no manner of means are women to be allowed to uncover and exhibit any part of their person, lest both fall — the men by being excited to look, they by drawing on themselves the eyes of men.[5]

Centuries of asceticism produced the attitude of contempt and horror expressed by the French monk Roger de Caen in *Carmen de Mundi Contemptu:*

> If her bowels and flesh were cut open, you would see what filth is covered by her white skin. If a fine crimson cloth covered a pile of foul dung, would anyone be foolish enough to love the dung because of it? . . . There is no plague which monks should dread more than woman; the soul's death.[6]

The Protestant Reformation, with its distaste for celibacy and its emphasis on the freedom of the individual believer, helped raise women out of the ascetic cesspool. But the idea that woman is somehow a dangerous temptress of the pure still surfaces in our churches today. One argument given to prove the impropriety of a woman preaching to a mixed audience reflects this idea: ''Any time men see a woman before them, they take notice of her body. This would cause sexual thoughts concerning her and temptations for the men. A good woman does not want to put herself in this position.''

Isn't it time we tossed out this prejudice against women? Let's stop punishing women for the excesses and distortions produced by asceticism. Let's find out what woman really is and treat her accordingly.

What Woman Is

I would like to enter a plea that women be recognized as human beings. Male and female hold much more in common than they do in difference.

Women have the same human needs as men

Women want to learn and have opportunities to express themselves. They want to be able as individuals to contribute whatever they can do well for the good of all. They want to be loved and respected and appreciated as unique human beings and not as functions or producers of a service or product. These are basic human needs that are experienced by men and women alike. That our varied experiences cause us to express ourselves and our needs differently should not make us think those needs are any less human or are not shared by both sexes.

Now let us look to the Bible. Does it present man and woman as having separate destinies or a shared humanity?

Woman was created as man's equal

One concludes from many sermons on creation that woman was the original factory reject. But since God is kind, He did not send her back; rather, He sold her at a reduced price and intended her for limited use. But in the first chapter of Genesis the creation of humankind is presented as one act. Man and woman were both given dominion over the earth; thus, the proper sphere of woman as well as man is the whole earth. There is no indication that they were not equal in ability, position, and authority.

The fact that Adam is spoken of in Genesis 2 as having been created first, whether a literal account of what took place or an example of the way God planned man and woman to relate to one another, does not argue for his being her superior in authority or ability or essence. God created living things in an ascending order of complexity. If order of creation means anything, it would have to mean Eve was superior because she was last. I'm not saying she was, but neither was she under Adam because of it.[7]

Woman was an equal sinner with man

If in fact Adam and Eve were created equals, as indicated in Genesis 1:26,27, and if they both knew they were commanded not to eat of the forbidden fruit, then they had to be held individually responsible for their actions. There is no evidence in the biblical account of the Fall that the sin of one was greater than that of the other. That they made different excuses for their actions is another matter. The sin was disobedience. They both disobeyed. They were expelled from the Garden together.

Woman was co-victim of the Fall

As woman shared in the sin, she shared in the results. But her share was not the same as man's — or was it? Man and woman are so interdependent that what affects one affects the other; therefore, we cannot say that only Adam suffered from having to till the ground and only Eve from her frequent childbirth. Woman also knows the labor of tilling the ground and feels the sweat run down her back. Man shares the results of woman's condition, for her many children weigh him down too. It is an endless circle, the human condition; and though the account in Genesis addresses woman and man separately, they share the sad results. They are co-victims.

Woman is co-heir to salvation

"Christ Jesus came into the world to save sinners" (1 Tim. 1:15).

"[In Christ] there is neither Jew nor Greek, . . . bond nor free, . . . male nor female" (Gal. 3:28 KJV).

"If therefore the Son shall make you free, you shall be free indeed" (John 8:36).

There are no segregated drinking fountains at the Water of Life. The woman of Samaria had equal access with the rich young ruler. We are all equal under the Cross.

Woman is co-receiver of spiritual gifts

The greatest gift of all is the Holy Spirit, whose presence within leads, comforts, and illumines the Bible for each believer. At Pentecost all received the Holy Spirit, men and women alike.

The lists of spiritual gifts in 1 Corinthians 12 and Ephesians 4 make no restriction as to who may receive them. First Corinthians 12:12,13 makes it clear that it refers to all believers, male and female. If these passages are directed toward all believers, then we cannot legitimately exclude women from receiving spiritual gifts. And we certainly cannot limit women to only a few, such as "helps," for never is there indication that women may receive only certain spiritual gifts, with all the rest reserved for men.

If woman is not singled out as somehow strangely different or exempted in regards to creation, the Fall, salvation, or spiritual gifts, then why can she not participate as freely as man in the church if the Holy Spirit leads her and enables her?

Let's apply all of Galatians 3:28: "There is neither Jew nor Greek, there is neither slave nor free man, there is neither male nor female; for you are all one in Christ Jesus." We no longer restrict leadership positions in the church to those who can buy their way in, as was once the case. We no longer believe in exempting people from full equality because of their skin color or ethnic background. Let's stop ignoring the full import of this passage and open up the church, all the way, for women too.

Notes

[1] Daphne A. Roe, M.D., *A Plague of Corn: The Social History of Pellagra* (Ithaca and London: Cornell University Press, 1973), p. x.

[2] Susan G. Bell, *Women: From the Greeks to the French Revolution* (Belmont, CA: Wadsworth Publishing Company, Inc., 1973), p. 18.

[3] Ibid., p. 122.

[4] Julia O'Faolain and Lauro Martines, eds., *Not in God's Image* (New York: Harper & Row, 1973), p. 132.

[5] Ibid., p. 133.

[6] Ibid., p. xiii.

[7] Jewish oral commentary developed an argument for the inferiority of woman based on the second account of creation in Genesis 2. For an explanation of Paul's possible reference to this Jewish rabbinical argument in 1 Timothy see chapter 5, pp. 74-79.

3

Three Threats to Hold Woman Down

3

Three Threats to Hold Woman Down

On you, ladies, depends, in a most important degree, the destiny of our country. In this day of disorder and turmoil, when the foundations of the great deep seem fast breaking up, and the flood of desolation threatening to roll over the whole face of society, it peculiarly devolves upon you to say what shall be the result. Yours it is to determine, whether the beautiful order of society . . . shall continue as it has been, to be a source of blessings to the world; or whether, despising all forms and distinctions, all boundaries and rules, society shall break up and become a chaos of disjointed and unsightly elements. Yours it is to decide, under God, whether we shall be a nation of refined and high minded Christians, or whether, rejecting the civilities of life, and throwing off the restraints of morality and piety, we shall become a fierce race of semi-barbarians, before whom neither order, nor honor, nor chastity can stand.

And be assured, ladies, if the hedges and borders of the social garden be broken up, the lovely vine, which now twines itself so gracefully upon the trellis, and bears such rich clusters, will be the first to fall and be trodden under foot. . . .[1]

Whenever women express doubts about their secondary position or move to act on an assumption of full personhood by doing whatever they *can do* and *wish to do* rather than what they are told they *should do* and *may do,* then three accusations rise up to point

29

threatening fingers at such boldness. Those threats are: "You will lose your femininity"; "You will destroy society (including the home and family)"; and "You deny the inspiration of the Scriptures." These threats deserve a closer look, for they are not always what they seem to be at first glance.

1. *"If you step outside your sphere (or role), you will lose your femininity."*

This threat was used years ago against the early women abolitionists for daring to speak publicly (as in the quote that opened this chapter). Today it is used to frighten women away from entering fields and using abilities labeled male.

Women aren't quite sure why this threat frightens them so. It carries implications women sense rather than think about. The primary implication is: "We males protect only feminine women (feminine by *our* definition). If you choose to step outside our protection, we will consider you legitimate prey for any man who wishes to abuse you. We will consider you as deviant, unlovable, and not worth protecting."

Angelina and Sarah Grimke's speeches on abolition prompted the following reaction in the Pastoral Letter of the Massachusetts Congregationalist Clergy, 1837:

> . . . but when she assumes the place and tone of man as a public reformer, our care and protection of her seem unnecessary; we put ourselves in self-defence against her; she yields the power which God has given her for protection, and her character becomes unnatural. If the vine, whose strength and beauty is to lean upon the trellis-work and half conceal its clusters, thinks to assume the independence and the overshadowing nature of the elm, it will not only cease to bear fruit, but fall in shame and dishonor into the dust.[2]

Even the issue of short hair has unleashed this threat.

> Oh women, what you have lost when you lost your femininity! When you bobbed your hair, you bobbed your character, too. Your rebellion against God's authority as exercised by husband and father, has a tendency, at least, to lose you all the things that women value most. If you want reverence and respect from good men, if you want protection and a good home and love and stedfast devotion, then I beg you to take a woman's place![3]

It is the threat of lost protection that strikes fear in the hearts of women, who know that as society now stands, they need the protection of someone when they are most vulnerable. Men have had the only power to protect them for so long that women have accepted that it is beyond their abilities to protect themselves and each other. This threat of lost femininity says, in effect, "We will consider you on the same level as prostitutes — something to use, abuse, and laugh at."

But what exactly is femininity? Can one lose it? If you ask an American about femininity, he will give you one kind of answer; if you ask an Iranian, he will probably give you an entirely different answer.

Femininity is an elusive quality women have that appeals to men. It is not to be defined, but enjoyed. The same is true of *masculinity, a quality men have that women appreciate.* Like the aroma of coffee or the fragrance of a meadow, it is indefinable but appreciated. You can make every effort to pin it down, but it will escape you. If you say strength, I can point to men who are loved for their vulnerability and charm. If you say decisiveness, I can point to men who cannot even make up their minds about which tie to wear and yet they are masculine.

What those who threaten loss of femininity are really saying is, "We define femininity by a set of things you can and cannot *do,* not by what you *are.*" And that is the fallacy. A woman cannot lose her femininity, because it is not a thing. Femininity is the very essence of a woman. And she cannot lose what she is.

Since femininity and masculinity are indefinable qualities, we tend to associate them with certain habits, mannerisms, and behavior and define them in terms of these. But that is not valid. Other cultures assign mannerisms and behavior differently. An action we call masculine could be called feminine somewhere else.

These roles and statuses, however, once developed, are then interpreted by the people within a culture as being genetically determined. And when the roles of males and females in strange societies or primitive cultures are observed to be different from our own, then we tend to assume that the other people are violating the God-given human nature of what men and women really ought to be.[4]

No one need fear the loss of a nature given to her by God. If God created her female, she is feminine. Her culture may say certain mannerisms, actions, and speech are feminine, another culture may say the reverse, but they are only learned responses. Basic femininity comes with the body — it's permanent.

This threat of lost femininity is really a paper tiger, but the threat of lost protection has real teeth. That threat we should face and deal with. We need to change laws that leave women without equal protection, such as rape laws. And we must insist that women be treated as full human beings instead of decorative but weak-minded playthings. Women must be allowed to be persons, not property, so that no woman need fear that she will be a legitimate target for abuse merely because she does what *she* thinks is right.

2. *"You will disrupt order and destroy society."*

This is an impressive threat, useful in combating any request for equal treatment made by any disadvantaged group. The implication is always that changes made by moves toward equality will be destructive changes. The threat is that all will come tumbling down and "we shall become a fierce race of semi-barbarians before whom neither order, nor honor, nor chastity can stand." This threat has been used especially against women when they dared to step outside the narrow place society has provided for them. It is said that women are the keystone in the arch of civilization, that they in their gentle, healing, restraining ways are all that keeps men from breaking out into barbarism and lawlessness. Women, the glue of society, must stay firmly in place.

It is true that giving freedom to disadvantaged groups creates changes. Societies in which there is a privileged or ruling class give great benefits to those on top of the hierarchical ladder. Many of those benefits cease when the disadvantaged group is given freedom.

If women are to be allowed equal pay, equal education, equal job opportunities, and equal voice in the church, then someone will have to move over and make room. Changes *will* come. But will those changes be destructive to the church and society or just to the favored positions of those who keep women down now?

When women struggled to gain the vote, it was said that suffrage would destroy order and the family, for it would take woman out of her place. When abolitionists worked for the emancipation of blacks, it was said that the black people were unable to contribute to society in any way other than as laborers; freeing them would destroy order and trigger degeneracy in society.

Instead of the predicted results, we have all reaped benefits from the abilities of blacks and women whose contributions would have been lost to us if they had been left to die in southern plantation cottonfields or bounded by kitchens and parlors. Is there an American who has not benefited from the work of George Washington Carver or a baby born whose parents would erase the work of Dr. Virginia Apgar, whose "Apgar Score" is widely used to evaluate a baby's overall condition within sixty seconds of birth, making it possible to predict — and often aid — the baby's chances for survival?

But where are the Virginia Apgars of the church? "I would have given her [the church] my head, my hand, my heart. She would not have them. She told me to go back and do crochet in my mother's drawing room," wrote Florence Nightingale.[5]

What body can work to full potential if half its members are bound with ropes and blinders so that full motion and vision are impossible? The body which is the church has bound its women in this way. Is there not room in God's church for all the members of His body to use everything He has given them?

Beneath all the fears, threats, and speculations of destruction lies the firm belief that there must be a rigid system of command in society. Many sincere and unselfish people actually believe there is a "divine order of command" and that somehow chaos will result if we violate it. They see hierarchy in both nature and human society. Chains of command seem to be necessary. These hierarchies are seen as unchangeable social formulae written by God and programed into our very nature.

It is assumed that all types of hierarchies are basically alike so that one can prove something about one hierarchy by looking at any other hierarchy. Thus analogies are used to prove things about a relationship or organization by looking at obvious features of another. "A ship needs a captain" is used to prove that "a family needs a ruler." But a family and ship are not the same. The assumption is that one can learn about governing families by studying how ships' crews are governed.

The mistake here is in using the method of analysis rather than the method of synthesis to study hierarchies. That is, we look at one or two hierarchies and assume that all hierarchies fit into the same pattern. Instead, we should look at the whole picture of hierarchical systems and discern the variables and invariables in such systems. Only then can we determine whether hierarchies are all the same. What are they based on? Are they flexible and changeable? What are their functions?

It is true that hierarchies occur naturally in nature and in groups of living things. It is *not* true that hierarchies are rigid systems in which every member has a predetermined place and function from which he may not move.

In the wild, one's place in a hierarchy is determined by how well he can do the job needed. If he cannot produce, he is either replaced or he dies, as may all who depend on the needed provision. The animal herd is in a state of constant change based on needs and resources. If the leader is incompetent to lead and protect the herd, he is replaced by a stronger and more competent leader; otherwise the herd suffers. The same is true of other members of the herd: scouts, nurses, young, etc. Each has a job, and all are interdependent. Their interdependence demands that they choose and rely upon only those who can fulfill the needed function. They are chosen by their sex only insofar as it affects demonstrated strength, speed, ability to bear young, skill, etc. Their positions in the hierarchy of the herd are based on *service they can give*.

But in the hierarchies of a highly organized human culture, there are many means for gaining position and maintaining it that have nothing to do with competence to do the job. The book *The Peter Principle*[6] makes it all too clear that we have ignored the natural selection of leaders and workers in our hierarchies. We attain status and the power that goes with it by use of money, acquaintance, prejudices, education (even when not applicable to the job), age, and sex, none of which may have anything to do with competence.

We cannot use the fact that there is spontaneous hierarchy in nature to support our argument for hierarchies based on foundations different from those in nature. The hierarchies we see in human society are too often corrupt, the product of a fallen humanity using power and position to oppress rather than serve. Corrupt hierarchy is a prerequisite to repression and oppression. Communism recognized this but mistook the cause as being ownership of property.

Natural hierarchy is a fluid, flexible correlation of abilities with needs and is based upon service to the other members of the group and the group as a whole.

The mutual submission of believers to each other in Ephesians 5:21 suggests similar relationships. Instead of rigid role playing, loving concern for each other guides our actions. Each one is free to contribute the gifts, abilities, and insights God has given him or her. There is no room for lording it over each other, no room for saying, "*I* will tell *you* what God wants you to do." Harmony and order are possible because the Holy Spirit is within us all and may direct each one according to His purposes. If our actions are motivated by mutual concern for each other and directed by the Holy Spirit, then we really are a "body" and we have true "oneness."

But this is not the way of the world.

Hierarchy based on the classical assumptions creates alienation, conflict, and frustration, along with other dysfunctional effects.[7]

Hierarchy means inequality in the distribution of valued goods whether in the form of power, money, prestige, or other social commodities.[8]

Persons at the bottom of the hierarchy live in a psychologically depressed area.[9]

Corrupt hierarchy rules with fear and force. It is rigid and punitive. It is restrictive and destructive, an outgrowth and expression of true worldliness.

We try to base our hierarchies or "order of command" in the church and family on some supposed "God-ordained position" in which woman is for all time under the governance of man. To prove this, we extract several portions of Scripture from their contexts and ignore all other evidence in the Bible contrary to this view. To do this, we must ignore God's original intent in creating man and woman as equals, Jesus' treatment of men and women as equals, equality in salvation, and equality in receiving spiritual gifts. We must also ignore the fact of our position as "adopted sons," a position which eliminates social or sexual advantage or disadvantage in the family of faith.

Again we make the mistake of studying the Bible by analysis before studying it by synthesis. We take isolated portions of Scripture and try to prove an all-encompassing truth when we should first take an overview of the broad sweep of Scripture so we can better see God's plan and our place in that plan. Only then can we look at the individual portions of Scripture and determine where they fit into God's scheme of things. The smallest part should be understood in relation to the whole. The practical should be understood in relation to the doctrinal.

Throughout Scripture, I see Christ reaching out to everyone and the Holy Spirit empowering all who believe. In the New Testament I see all believers participating.

We need to look again at those verses that have been used to prove a divine chain of command and see how they fit with the whole. And if they do not fit as we have interpreted them in the past, what do they mean?

Rather than worry about maintaining a rigid hierarchy of command with male always above female, we should reinstate the

God-directed decree "in Christ there is no male and female." We should free both men and women to be, under the Holy Spirit's direction, all that God would have them to be. Then the church, the family, and the society will have the use of all the talents and abilities of its members doing the work they are best able to do.

It will not destroy anything good. It will profit us all.

3. *"You are denying the inspiration of the Bible."*

This accusation is an all-purpose silencer. It is most useful to those with credentials as Bible scholars. It is a form of spiritual one-upmanship. What they are really saying is, "If you disagree with my interpretation of the Bible, I am going to try to frighten you into thinking it is the only possible interpretation God will allow." It sounds impressive to someone not sure she or he can speak as authoritatively as the one making the accusation.

The technique is used frequently. John R. Rice used it in his book *Bobbed Hair, Bossy Wives, and Women Preachers:*

> Yes, these are matters of controversy, whether a woman sins in cutting her hair, whether a woman must be subject to her husband, ruled by him, or be equal with him in authority, and whether a woman may be permitted to take the place of authority and leadership in church affairs just as men do, to be a pastor or evangelist. These are controversial matters. But note this, that the controversy is never about *what the Bible says on these questions*. There is no controversy there, for the Bible is so plain that there can be no dispute.[10]

Charles Ryrie uses the technique in the conclusion of his book, *The Place of Women in the Church*. First he admits he does not have enough evidence, but then he says no other conclusions than his are valid, because to conclude otherwise would deny Bible inspiration.

> Many desired things are lacking in the evidence and in the final picture, but since all the evidence has been presented, one must be content with the conclusions. One more question must be asked . . . "what is the ideal of woman? What could we call the complete development and full blossoming of woman's life?" It is a question which is much agitated in all branches of the Christian church today, and it is a question which has presented itself again and

again as this study was being made. Those who share this author's view of inspiration will answer it by saying that in the inspired writings we have the mind of God concerning the full development of women. And this will mean subordination and honor in the home, silence and helpfulness in the church, according to the teaching and pattern of the New Testament. At least that ought to be the answer of all who believe in the divine inspiration and authority of the Scriptures, for if these teachings concerning women are not authoritative then what teachings in the New Testament are?[11]

Some pastors use the same method to silence opponents to their views. Few lay Christians care to try to defend their own interpretation against such statements. Who are they anyway? And if that layperson is also a woman, she has even less chance to challenge successfully such an authoritative statement. Women are supposed to keep quiet and work in the background — to be seen but not heard.

Every pastor knows there are principles of Bible interpretation and that these principles are used to weigh differing interpretations of questionable passages. He knows many men who differ with him concerning the interpretation of passages on Christian practice, men whose loyalty to the doctrine of inspiration he does not doubt. Then why try to make everyone in his congregation accept his own interpretation and imply that they don't believe the Bible if they disagree? Perhaps such a man mistakes conformity for unity and thinks he is a good shepherd if he makes all his sheep the same.

Commentators do not agree on the interpretations of the passages referring to women. On some passages there are almost as many interpretations as there are commentators.

We must not be confused by the words *inspiration* and *interpretation*. To claim the *inspiration* of the Scriptures is to believe that what the Bible says is true — that it is God's written Word to us. *Interpretation* involves explaining what this Word means to us on a human level. Therefore, interpretation leaves room for human error, and we must recognize in others' pulling of spiritual or educational rank that they are not infallible in their interpretation of Scripture.

It is not hard to believe that the Bible has sometimes been interpreted narrowly to support a private view or bias. But some of the misuses Scripture has been put to in the past are almost beyond comprehension. In the next chapter we will look at some of those shameful episodes in the history of Bible *mis*interpretation.

Notes

[1]Aileen S. Kraditor, ed., *Up From the Pedestal* (Chicago: Quadrangle Books, 1968), p. 50.

[2]Ibid., p. 51.

[3]John R. Rice, *Bobbed Hair, Bossy Wives, and Women Preachers* (Wheaton, IL: Sword of the Lord Publishers, 1941), pp. 78,79.

[4]David Moberg, "Sociologist's Perspective on Woman's Role and Status," (tape) Denver Seminary Conference on Women, 1974.

[5]Russell C. Prohl, *Woman in the Church* (Grand Rapids: Eerdmans, 1957), p. 77.

[6]Laurence J. Peter and Raymond Hull, *The Peter Principle* (New York: William Morrow and Co., 1969).

[7]Arnold S. Tannenbaum, et al., *Hierarchy in Organizations: An International Comparison* (San Francisco: Jossey-Bass, 1974), p. 5.

[8]Ibid., p. 2.

[9]Ibid., p. 10.

[10]Rice, *Bobbed Hair, Bossy Wives, and Women Preachers*, p. 9.

[11]Charles Ryrie, *The Place of Women in the Church* (New York: Macmillan, 1958), p. 146.

4

Ammunition for Repression:
Misuse of Scripture in the Past

4

Ammunition for Repression: Misuse of Scripture in the Past

> It is because they have mistaken the dawn for a conflagration that theologians have so often been foes of light.[1]

I do not enjoy writing a chapter like this. It disturbs, even horrifies me when I read how the Book I love has been misused to hurt people.

But we must recognize the danger in believing that sincerity and good intentions are enough to prevent *our* misusing the Bible; and we must also avoid complacently thinking that just because our practices are of long standing, they must be right. Some of the abuses I shall mention lasted for centuries. We are now convinced they were wrong.

I include this chapter in the hope that we can see the mistakes of others and examine why they fell into them so we may avoid them ourselves, particularly as we look at the Bible and its teaching about women.

THE INQUISITION

The medieval church was afflicted with corruption and heresy. It considered the corruption regrettable, but the heresy irreconcilable.

Heresy consisted of any belief that differed from the official

43

doctrine of the Catholic church. The church reasoned that since it was Christ's body, there could be no spiritual life outside that body. Those who departed from official church teaching were in danger of damnation because they were removing themselves from the body. Further, it was thought that all things had their proper place in God's order, and the church was the ultimate ruler over all the earth. This made all belief subject to church approval, whether on religion, science, medicine, or human nature. Those who differed from official doctrine on any subject were guilty of heresy.

So the Holy Office of Inquisition was founded to search out heretics and, hopefully, bring them back into the fold. The Inquisition is infamous for its use of torture to gain confessions and persuade heretics to renounce their beliefs. The inquisitors justified their methods with Bible texts as interpreted by Augustine. Early in the Christian Era Augustine had used Luke 14:23 to prove that the use of force with heretics was biblical:

> You are of the opinion that no one should be compelled to follow after righteousness: and yet you read that the householder said to his servants, "Whomsoever ye shall find, compel them to come in." You also read how he who was at first Saul, and afterwards Paul, was compelled, by the great violence with which Christ coerced him, to know and to embrace the truth.[2]

This passage and others like Proverbs 27:6 — "Faithful are the wounds of a friend" — were used to justify the punishment of the body to save the soul.

GALILEO

Probably the most famous victim of the Inquisition was the astronomer Galileo Galilei. He became convinced by observations through his telescope that the earth moved around the sun. For this belief he was punished.

The church taught that the way to learn about the mysteries of the natural world was not by observation, but by assembling passages of Scripture on the subject and then drawing conclusions by careful theological reasoning based on those passages. By such reasoning theologians had developed a view of all creation assembled in a "divine order." Everything and everyone had a fixed place in this scheme. All beings and phenomena, from angels to rain, were accounted for in this manner with such texts as Psalm 104:5,13 and Isaiah 51:13,16. This divine order was so firmly based on biblical texts that to question any part of it was considered blasphemy.

Within the system, man was the center of creation and all was made for him. The church ruled over all the earth. Sun, moon, and stars were fixed to transparent spheres and revolved about the stationary earth. The transparent spheres were turned by angels, and rain was released from actual windows in heaven which were opened and closed by the angels. To claim, as Galileo did, that the earth did not stand still with the whole universe revolving around it was to demolish the entire system and to deny the inspiration of the Bible.

The Copernican Theory, that the earth turned on its axis and revolved with the other planets around the sun, had been advanced earlier and labeled heresy. But it had been only a theory, an interesting idea. Now, with his telescope, Galileo proved it to be true.

Plots, harassment, and accusations were directed against him. Though he tried to prove that his observations were not inconsistent with the Bible and to defend his own personal faith in God, he was accused of atheism and efforts to destroy Christian belief. Finally, he was summoned by the dreaded Inquisition. After repeated threats of torture, he gave in. The statement he signed declared all his discoveries about the movement of the earth to be false. He was exiled from his family and friends. Even his dying wish to be buried in his family plot was denied, and no monument was allowed over his grave.

The Copernican system was then denounced throughout the Christian world. Catholic and Protestant alike worked to root out Galileo's influence. Men from Luther and Calvin to Puritan John Owen and Methodist John Wesley believed his teaching to be contrary to Scripture and spoke against it.

The earth still moved. But knowledge of the true nature of the universe and scientific investigation in general were successfully stifled for centuries as a result of the action against Galileo.

WITCHES

During times of disaster and social unrest, people look for scapegoats to blame for their troubles. Many Jews were killed for causing the plagues that raged through Europe during the Middle Ages. People thought the Jews secretly poisoned Christians' wells, causing the sickness.

The Inquisition eventually turned to the work of apprehending the witches who were causing storms, crop failures, stillborn infants, and all kinds of other disasters.

Two Dominicans set about writing a guidebook for witch inquisitors. In 1486 they published the *Malleus Maleficarum*[3] *(Hammer of Witches),* one of the most obscene books ever written. This book guided inquisitors throughout Europe as they tortured and burned hundreds of thousands of people.[4]

It was not proper to burn a suspected witch without a confession of guilt, so torture was used until such a confession could be obtained. Then more torture was applied until the witch implicated others as witches. People confessed to all manner of impossible feats, anything suggested to them, to stop the torture. Confession brought release, but of only one kind — death. Even a confessed and repentant witch was burned or hanged. The inquisitors used Exodus 22:18 ("Thou shalt not suffer a witch to live," KJV) to show their obligation to find and destroy them.

Roman Catholics were not alone in appropriating this verse for killing witches. Protestants also felt the call to search and destroy. They did not want to be less zealous than Catholics in fighting evil. King James of England even wrote a book[5] on the subject of witches, being convinced a witch had caused a storm at sea that endangered his bride as she sailed to England.

For two hundred years the witch mania fed on the misuse of this Bible passage.

MEDICINE

The forward march of medicine has been bruised and battered on the wall of Bible misinterpretation more than once. I will relate only three of the many instances of misplaced zeal that for a time succeeded in denying relief to many in the name of God.

Since the medieval method of determining truth on any subject was by theological reasoning based on assembled Bible texts, rather than by observation of the subject under study, it is only natural that medicine would suffer the same fate as Galileo's astronomy. Theologians and churchmen opposed medical advances because they saw the basis of their medical beliefs threatened. They did not realize that it was their *interpretation* of the Bible that was threatened, not the Bible itself. They had made the common mistake of locking their interpretation into a rigid man-made system. And when their system was threatened, they thought the Bible was too.

Childbed Fever

Childbirth had always been a hazardous event for mother and child. But the filthy conditions in hospitals before the discovery of microbes made childbirth even more dangerous. In the large Allgemeines Krankenhaus in Vienna in 1844, almost one mother in ten died of childbed fever.[6] Many reasons were suggested for this. Some thought the disease was caused by excessive modesty — women not wanting to be examined by male doctors (the disease rate was much lower in the clinic run by midwives). Or perhaps it was caused by bad water, food, or poor ventilation. Others believed the women died because it was God's will that they die — a result of the curse on women in Genesis 3:16.

But a young doctor named Semmelweis discovered the real reason. Though he spent long hours in the autopsy room searching for a clue to this puzzling killer, no clue appeared. All he could determine was that formerly healthy women suddenly developed a fever and died within hours of an overwhelming internal infection.

He stumbled on the answer when a fellow physician died as a result of a scalpel cut on his finger received while performing an autopsy. Semmelweis suddenly realized his colleague's septicemia was identical to his own patients' childbed fever. Then he knew. Something was being transmitted from the autopsy rooms, on the doctors' hands, to women in labor. But it was not so easy to convince others of what he was now sure: doctors were killing their own patients with dirty hands.

Semmelweis wrote a book to explain his theory. It was scorned. Obstetricians around the world ridiculed his ideas. Dr. Charles D. Meigs, a noted Philadelphia obstetrician, attributed deaths from childbed fever to "justification of Providence; a judgment instituted to remind us of the sin committed by the mother of the race."[7] Many devout physicians held the same view. They believed that the words of Genesis 3:16, "I will greatly multiply your pain in childbirth, in pain you shall bring forth children," sealed the fate of women in labor, and nothing they could do would change it.

Failure was too much for Semmelweis, who regarded his colleagues as murderers, slaughtering innocent women with some matter carried on their hands from dead bodies and sick patients. He finally broke under the strain, was confined to an insane asylum, and died.

He was right, of course, and was eventually honored posthumously. But many more mothers died before doctors would believe Semmelweis and give up their other theories, including the theory which held that the mothers must die in fulfillment of Genesis 3:16.

Painkillers in Childbirth

Women ran into the problem of misinterpretation of Genesis 3:16 again when ether and chloroform were introduced into obstetrical practice.

Natural anesthetics, such as henbane and opiates, had been used in antiquity but were later forbidden by the church. Use of painkillers was considered a lack of faith in God at best and at worst sorcery and witchcraft. A lady of rank, Eufame MacLayne, was tried in Scotland in 1591 for hiring a midwife to provide her with "a certain medicine for the relief of pain in childbirth contrary to Divine law and in contempt of the Crown." Eufame's twin infants were taken from her, and she was burned to death for her offense.[8]

In the middle of the nineteenth century Dr. James Y. Simpson, professor of obstetrics at the University of Glasgow, published his results with chloroform in a number of especially difficult births. He was immediately attacked from all sides. An article in an Edinburgh medical journal in 1847 protested:

> Pain during operations is, in the majority of cases, even desirable; its prevention or annihilation is, for the most part, hazardous to the patient. In the lying-in chamber, nothing is more true than this; pain is the mother's safety, its absence, her destruction. Yet there are those bold enough to administer the vapor of Ether, even at this critical juncture, forgetting it has been ordered that "in sorrow shall she bring forth."[9]

Clergymen as well as doctors denounced him for using anesthesia on obstetrical patients.

Fortunately Dr. Simpson was learned in theology and the Bible as well as obstetrics, and he answered his critics by showing from Scripture that to aid those in pain *was* God's will, and the supposed "curse" was not at all what his accusers thought it to be.

Relief from pain in difficult labor is available to women today. Most are not even aware there ever was a theological battle to deny it to them.

Smallpox

Smallpox hardly raises a ripple of interest now, but in eighteenth-century Europe fear of smallpox was definitely justified. It is estimated that during that century fifty million people died from smallpox in Europe.[10] A repulsive disease that produced blisters of pus, which became running sores, it often left its survivors with deeply pock-scarred faces.

In 1721 Lady Mary Wortley Montague brought home to England a crude method of inoculation against smallpox which she had seen practiced in Turkey. Pus was collected from sores on victims with light cases of the disease and applied to opened veins in healthy subjects. Later, Edward Jenner, an English physician, improved the procedure by using pus from cowpox eruptions. Though the procedure was successful in immunizing people against the disease, it sometimes made them quite ill, and some even died. But for the population at large, it was a vast improvement over no immunity at all. The death rate from smallpox dropped drastically wherever widespread inoculation was carried out.

Some clergymen welcomed the discovery, but others denounced it as evil and contrary to God's will and Word. The practice of inoculation was condemned by French theologians of the Sorbonne[11] as well as English, Scottish, and American preachers. Sermons such as "The Dangerous and Sinful Practice of Inoculation"[12] presented sickness and disease as divine judgment and inoculation as an effort to "baffle that divine Judgment," bringing even greater judgment from God.[13] One Bible passage quoted to support this view was Hosea 6:1: "Come, let us return to the LORD. For He has torn us, but He will heal us; He has wounded us, but He will bandage us."

Fortunately not all clergymen were opposed to inoculation. Many of the Puritan preachers in New England were supporters. The famous pastor and theologian Jonathan Edwards died as a result of his smallpox inoculation, as did his daughter, the mother of Aaron Burr.[14]

Eventually the furor died down and inoculation became an accepted method of disease prevention, saving millions of people from misery and death.

SLAVERY

Slavery is an old practice. In ancient times, it was a practical matter. The conqueror had the right to the labor of the conquered. And sometimes during famines, parents sold their children into slavery to keep them from starving to death.

But nineteenth-century American slaveholders could not adequately defend slavery by appealing to its practicality. Too many Christian consciences were pricked by the contrast between slavery and basic tenets of Christianity. The priesthood of the believer, equality before God, and personal responsibility of believers made Christianity incompatible with slavery.

To still the doubts and discredit abolitionists working to free the slaves, pro-slavery clergymen sought to prove that slavery was biblical. The Presbyterian theologian Robert Lewis Dabney presented the strategy in 1851:

> Here is our policy then, to push the Bible argument continually, to drive Abolitionism to the wall, to compel it to assume an anti-Christian position.[15]

One of their tactics was to imply that abolitionists rejected the authority of Scripture in favor of human reasonings.

> In answering this question, as a Church, let it be distinctly borne in mind that the only rule of judgment is the written word of God. The Church knows nothing of the intuitions of reason or the deductions of philosophy, except those reproduced in the Sacred Canon. She has a positive constitution in the Holy Scriptures, and has no right to utter a single syllable upon any subject except as the Lord puts words in her mouth. She is founded, in other words, upon express *revelation*. Her creed is an authoritative testimony of God, and not a speculation, and what she proclaims, she must proclaim with the infallible certitude of faith, and not with the hesitating assent of an opinion. . . . Now, we venture to assert that if men had drawn their conclusions upon this subject only from the Bible, it would no more have entered into any human head to denounce slavery as a sin, than to denounce monarchy, aristocracy or poverty. The truth is, men have listened to what they falsely considered as primitive intuitions, or as necessary deductions from primitive cognitions, and then have gone to the Bible to confirm the crochets of their vain philosophy.[16]

Many texts from both Old (e.g., Leviticus 25:44-46) and New Testaments were quoted to support slavery. Matthew 8:9-13 tells of a certain centurion with servants (taken to mean slaves) who was praised by Christ with nothing said against his slaveholdings. Luke 17:7-10 contains a parable in which Christ talks about slavery without censuring it. First Corinthians 7:20-24 tells slaves as well as free persons to abide in the calling they are in and care nothing for it. Several passages refer to the behavior of believing slaves toward their masters, such as Ephesians 6:5-8 and

1 Timothy 6:1,2. The conclusion was, then, that slavery was recognized and regulated under Christianity, but never criticized as a practice.

Bishop John England explained the position of the slave and master in the *United States Catholic Miscellany* and found Christian equality to be in spiritual matters only.

> The slave is taught from the most powerful motives to be faithful, patient, obedient and contented, and the master is taught that though despotism may pass unpunished on earth it will be examined into at the bar of heaven: . . . the servant must readily and cheerfully pay him homage and perform his behests on earth, yet they may be on an equality in heaven.[17]

The argument of approval by silence was put forth by Baptist Dr. Richard Furman:

> Had the holding of slaves been a moral evil, it cannot be supposed that the inspired Apostles, who feared not the faces of men, and were ready to lay down their lives in the cause of their God, would have tolerated it, for a moment, in the Christian Church. . . . In proving this subject justifiable by Scriptural authority, its morality is also proved; for the Divine Law never sanctions immoral actions.[18]

He also uses the old "divine order" argument to support slavery.

> The Christian golden rule, of doing to others, as we would they should do to us, has been urged as an unanswerable argument against holding slaves. But surely this rule is never to be urged against that order of things, which the Divine government has established; nor do our desires become a standard to us, under this rule unless they have a due regard to justice, propriety and the general good.[19]

So, by a multitude of Bible passages it was proved that slavery was not only condoned and regulated by God, but was part of His plan for society.

The apologists for slavery even went so far as to say that it was for the best spiritual interest of the slaves that they had been stolen from their own native land, for now they could be reached for God. But as a fugitive slave wrote in 1847:

In Missouri, and as far as I have any knowledge of slavery in the other states, the religious teaching consists of teaching the slave that he must never strike a white man; that God made him for a slave; and that, when whipped, he must not find fault — for the Bible says, "He that knoweth his master's will and doeth it not, shall be beaten with many stripes!" And slaveholders find such religion very profitable to them.[20]

There are striking parallels between many of the arguments for slavery and those for the submission of women to men. It was a recognition of these similarities that sparked the early feminist movement among women abolitionists.

We ask ourselves how all these abuses of the Bible could happen. How could people who were upright, even theologically trained, use God's Word as a club to beat down others? Is it possible to avoid such mistakes?

In every case, we find that there *were* Christians who realized the Bible was not being accurately and justly used. They often spoke out at a risk to their own lives and property. So those mistakes were *not* inevitable.

The misuse of Bible passages was possible only by violating sound principles of Bible interpretation. Sometimes it was to support practices that were already common before the church entered the situation. At other times it was to obtain power or wealth or was an attempt to justify evil actions. In still other instances it was the result of a rigid adherence to a system thought up by human beings and considered to be the only one God would allow. But all of those misuses could have been avoided if the church had used sound interpretative principles and allowed freedom within itself for diverse views and honest questioning. tioning.

In the next chapter we will look at some principles of Bible interpretation and then at those passages which have been used to keep women from full participation in the church and society.

Notes

[1]A. D. White, *A History of the Warfare of Science With Theology in Christendom* (New York: Dover Publications, 1960), vol. I, p. 432.

[2]Frederick A. Norwood, *Strangers and Exiles* (Nashville: Abingdon, 1969), vol. I, p. 107.

[3]H. R. Hays, *The Dangerous Sex* (New York: Pocket Books, 1965), pp. 141-44; William Woods, *A Casebook of Witchcraft* (New York: Putnam, 1974), pp. 58-60.

[4]Jeffrey Burton Russell, *Witchcraft in the Middle Ages* (Ithaca: Cornell University Press, 1972), p. 39.

[5]*Daemonologie*, excerpts quoted in William Woods, *A Casebook of Witches*.

[6]Donald T. Atkinson, *Magic, Myth, and Medicine* (Cleveland: World, 1956), pp. 273,274.

[7]Ibid., p. 274.

[8]Bernard Seeman, *Man Against Pain* (Philadelphia: Chilton, 1962), p. 96. Also White, *A History of the Warfare,* vol. II, p. 62.

[9]Seeman, *Man Against Pain,* p. 123.

[10]Robert Reid, *Microbes and Men* (New York: Dutton, 1975), p. 10.

[11]White, *A History of the Warfare,* vol. II, p. 55.

[12]Ibid.

[13]Ibid., p. 56.

[14]Elisabeth D. Dodds. *Marriage to a Difficult Man* (Philadelphia: Westminster Press, 1971), pp. 195-97.

[15]H. Shelton Smith, Robert T. Handy, and Lefferts A. Loetscher, *American Christianity* (New York: Scribners, 1963), vol. II, p. 177.

[16]Ibid., pp. 206,207.

[17]Ibid., p. 204.

[18]Ibid., p. 185.

[19]Ibid.

[20]Julius Lester, *To Be A Slave* (New York: Dell, 1968), p. 78.

5

Those Problem Passages

5

Those Problem Passages

Traditionally, certain Bible passages have been used to restrict women to a narrow place in the church and society. These verses are easily dealt with by those who do not believe in the inspiration of Scripture. They simply disregard them as the work of misogynists or writers with patriarchal bias. The Bible believer has a real problem in knowing what to do with these passages. Should we take them at face value and try to observe them to the letter? This results in action conflicting with other Scripture. Shall we try to interpret them culturally and say they were for then but not for now? Shall we do a little of both and hope for the best? Or is there another alternative? I suggest that we try to discover what the passages were attempting to teach the people to whom they were written, determine the principles implicit in them, and then apply those principles to our lives.

In actual practice most of these verses are interpreted by the individual pastor to suit his own ideas on the subject of women. If he feels strongly that women should be restricted, he will be firm in interpreting the passages literally and applying them to today. If he isn't bothered by the idea of women having a great deal of freedom, he may ignore these verses. When asked about them, he might make a joke and dismiss the question with as little explana-

57

tion as possible. Women are left with the idea that the less asked about this subject the better. Many women decide to remain ignorant in that area and just do the best they can with the freedom they are allowed.

As I remarked before, little digging has been done on these verses, and what has been done is not usually made available to women in the churches for the simple reason that it is not seen as an important area of study by most men in the ministry. And why ask for trouble by discussing it?

But the interpretation of these verses *is* important to women, because their personal lives and service in the body of Christ are regulated and bounded by these verses. They deserve careful study. And the results of that study should be made available to every woman in the church.

It is with this conviction in mind that I present the material in this section. I do not claim to know exactly how each of these passages of Scripture should be interpreted. One or two passages are so difficult to explain that virtually no Bible scholar will say he has the final answer. Some present problems that perhaps will only be solved when we talk to those to whom the letters were originally written and they say, ''Oh, that refers to so-and-so and the problem we had then. You wouldn't understand that unless you were there.''

But there are principles of interpretation anyone can follow to decide upon the probable meaning or meanings of a passage. These principles are recognized by all who seriously study the Bible.

PRINCIPLES OF BIBLE INTERPRETATION

1. Always interpret a verse in agreement with its context (its surrounding verses or chapters). That is, the meaning of the part must be consistent with the whole.

2. Interpret a passage in the light of its probable meaning to the persons for whom it was originally written.

3. When interpreting a passage, consider the customs and events taking place when it was written.

4. Interpret a passage in the light of all other Scripture.

5. Do not use an obscure passage to disprove one with clear and obvious meaning.

6. Interpret a passage according to the best use of the original language.

7. Interpret social teaching in line with doctrinal teaching.

8. If there is a principle set forth in the passage, do not interpret or apply the passage in such a manner as to deny or reverse the principle.

9. Interpret the unknown in accordance with the known.

10. Do not interpret a passage in such a way as to make it deny what we know to be true of God from other Scripture.[1]

There is practically nothing in the Bible that does not require some interpretation. Take the command "Thou shalt not kill." Does this mean one should never kill anything? Interpretation involves weighing what we already know about God, the vehicle for the words, the context, and the social climate. We must try to determine what God is really trying to tell us. Often we miss the kernel of truth and become obsessed with the shell. Or we try to extract a divine law where principle only is indicated.

In interpretation we must assume certain things, but we must not assume unnecessarily. Should we assume that since God revealed Himself to a nation with a patriarchal form of family life that He approves of only a patriarchal system? Can we assume that since God has prospered American Christians to the point where they can send missionaries to many other cultures that He is thereby approving our culture and wishes us to teach it along with Christianity? Many missionaries have mingled the two to the detriment of their converts and the gospel.

Beware of illustration reversal. Taking an illustration in Scripture and turning it around to make what is illustrated prove the illustration, instead of vice versa, is faulty interpretation. We would not assume that since God uses a sower sowing grain by hand as an illustration of preaching the good news that God approves of sowing seed only in this manner and those using mechanical seeders are acting contrary to His will. We must also recognize that illustrations are only devices used to make something clear to the people spoken to, not perfect examples of divine truth. We must try to determine what that truth is, not rigidly duplicate the conditions in the illustration.

We, as evangelicals who believe in the divine inspiration of the Bible, are quick to emphasize that the very words are inspired. And this is good. But like all good things it is capable of misuse. We sometimes isolate Scripture from its surrounding verses and try to prove things with individual words that a study of their context would show us was not the original intention of the writer. If we take a word like *submit* or *head* and build a case on it that runs contrary to the meaning of the context, our action is not consistent with our belief in inspiration, for we are making the word mean something God did not intend.

PROBLEM PASSAGES

Genesis 3:16

> To the woman He said, "I will greatly multiply your pain in childbirth, in pain you shall bring forth children; yet your desire shall be for your husband, and he shall rule over you."

This passage, once used to deny women the use of anesthesia and painkillers in childbirth has had far-reaching misuse. It has been generally interpreted as proof that women were to be inescapably under the domination of men, that it was God's "order of things," and that this order could not be ignored without throwing the whole social system out of kilter. It also is used to support man's right to rule over woman politically, financially, socially, educationally, and sexually.

The problem with these interpretations is that basically they ignore other Scripture, primarily the first chapter of Genesis, in which we can see God's intention toward humankind in His original creation. The restrictive interpretations of Genesis 3:16 must also ignore all other Scripture that gives woman equal freedom with man.

It is interesting to notice the selective use of the results of the Fall by many Bible teachers. We are often told that this passage proves woman's subordination and that it applies to all women for all time. Yet in the same passage, just previous to the message to Eve, Adam is told that he will earn his bread by the sweat of his brow. How often is that preached on as unchangeable?

These instructions or warnings are plainly *results* of the Fall, not God's initial purpose in creation. If this is to be applied as God's unalterable will for woman, then the results of the Fall upon man should also be regarded as God's unalterable will, which means that he should do nothing to make his toil easier or alleviate the problems of thorns and thistles. Even antiperspirants would be wrong, as well as all efforts to prolong life, because they frustrate the sentence of death.

Obviously a consistent application of these verses as the unalterable will of God is absurd. They are the *results* of the Fall. Our God is a God of grace, and since the Fall He has been progressively working to nullify these results. The ideal is to be found in Genesis 1 and 2, not in Genesis 3.

There is no indication of a subordination of woman in the beginning. God says in Genesis 1:28ff. that He gives *them* dominion over the earth. No indication of man's position of authority appears until after the Fall. If we take the pronouncements of God in verses 14 through 19 as a curse from God to be unwaveringly applicable to all mankind, then it does not make sense, because not all women have children, not all mothers have painful childbirth, not all women have husbands, not all men eat the herb of the field, not all eat by the sweat of their brow, and not all men have died (e.g., Elijah).

But if we interpret these pronouncements as the natural consequences of the upset in the world caused by the Fall and the entrance of sin (including its chain-reaction effects), they do make sense, for all these things happen to humankind and would not happen but for the Fall. And all these things are modified or changed by God's grace and provision. So, we should not interpret these pronouncements as God's decree that it *must* be so, but as His informing Adam and Eve that this was the direction things would go. These were the far-reaching effects of what they had done.

But God in His kindness and mercy began immediately to provide for the eventual and complete release from their dilemma with the promise of a Savior (the woman's seed that would bruise the serpent's head). Christ came to correct the results of the Fall, not to reinforce them.

We thank God for all good gifts. And those gifts often serve to modify or overrule some of the bad effects of the Fall. The tragic results of the Fall should never be taken as patterns to follow or institutionalize in the family, church, or society.

Instead of looking to the Fall for our example, let's look to Christ and His dealings with men and women. He dealt with them as equals whom He cared about intensely and impartially. Jesus Himself pointed to the first intention of God when asked about the uneven relationship of man and woman in marriage and divorce. He said, "From the beginning it has not been this way" (Matt. 19:8). We too should work to restore the original relationship between man and woman — equality in dominion and responsibility, both to God and to each other.

Another view of this passage is that the domination of man over woman was only to last until the birth of the promised Savior. After Christ the relationship of the sexes was to be one of equality. The trouble with this interpretation is that it again is selective and ignores man's working by the sweat of his brow and the ground's bringing forth thorns and thistles.

According to Dr. Lee Anna Starr in *The Bible Status of Woman*,[2] the word *desire* ("your desire shall be for your husband") should be translated "turning." Thus translated, it would read: "your turning shall be toward your husband." With this rendering it reflects the dependence woman would increasingly find herself experiencing as the effects of the Fall progressed.

Dr. Starr's reasons for insisting on the change are: All ancient versions of the Old Testament render the Hebrew word as "turning" or "will turn" or "to turn away." In the sixteenth century an Italian Dominican monk named Pagnino published his translation of the Hebrew Bible. Influenced by the teachings of the Talmud, he translated the word "lust." With the exception of the two

Vulgate versions, every English translation since the time of Pagnino has followed his example, making the word import lust or sensual desire.

1 Corinthians 11:3-16

> [3]But I want you to understand that Christ is the head of every man, and the man is the head of a woman, and God is the head of Christ. [4]Every man who has something on his head while praying or prophesying, disgraces his head. [5]But every woman who has her head uncovered while praying or prophesying, disgraces her head; for she is one and the same with her whose head is shaved. [6]For if a woman does not cover her head, let her also have her hair cut off; but if it is disgraceful for a woman to have her hair cut off or her head shaved, let her cover her head. [7]For a man ought not to have his head covered, since he is the image and glory of God; but the woman is the glory of man. [8]For man does not originate from woman, but woman from man; [9]for indeed man was not created for the woman's sake, but woman for the man's sake. [10]Therefore the woman ought to have a symbol of authority on her head, because of the angels. [11]However, in the Lord, neither is woman independent of man, nor is man independent of woman. [12]For as the woman originates from the man, so also the man has his birth through the woman; and all things originate from God. [13]Judge for yourselves; is it proper for a woman to pray to God with head uncovered? [14]Does not even nature itself teach you that if a man has long hair, it is a dishonor to him, [15]but if a woman has long hair, it is a glory to her? For her hair is given to her for a covering. [16]But if one is inclined to be contentious, we have no other practice, nor have the churches of God.

This passage is usually a foundation stone in the proofs for a divine "chain of command," in which God the Father is at the top, Christ the Son is next, then comes man, and finally woman. All orders and responsibilities go in descending and ascending order respectively.

This passage has also been used to legislate a head covering for women when praying or speaking in church. Until recently, Roman Catholic women were expected to cover their heads in church, if only with a handkerchief. Amish women wear head coverings both in and out of church. Other groups will let women go without a hat or veil but insist on long hair as a head covering.

Some say woman protects the angels by covering her head because she thus reaffirms her divinely ordained position under man's authority. They even go so far as to say that the angels might be tempted to sin like Lucifer if they had to watch women praying or prophesying with uncovered heads.

If subordination of woman is spiritual and extends to all her relationships, if all her life she must be under the command of some man — whether father, husband, or son — then she never attains the equality and freedom Christianity has claimed to give her. If she is under total authority of a husband when married, but takes her instruction directly from God when single, then marriage would seem to be a step away from God.

There is reason to doubt that what is meant by "head" in this passage is the same as our idea of "leader." The biblical word here is more like "source" or "origin." There is a play on the word *head* in this passage in which it is used figuratively as "source" or "origin" and also literally as a part of the body representing honor and respect. This is then related to covering or uncovering the head as a means of honor or dishonor.

In many cultures body parts have differing degrees of respectability and honor. In the East one eats with the right hand and performs toilet functions with the left; thus, the right hand is more honorable than the left. The term for the left hand in Latin is *sinister*, the "bad hand." The head is most honored, the feet most dishonored throughout the East. This is why King Mongkut, in the book *Anna and the King of Siam,* allowed no one's head to be higher than his own. Servants were required to crawl to serve him when he was seated or reclining lest they be higher in honor. It is a similar use of the word *head* that we have here, indicating the seat of respectability and honor.

Verse 5 refers to women with short hair as being disgraceful. Later, verses 14 and 15 state that nature itself teaches that it is a shame for men to have long hair and a glory for women to have long hair. But nature as we think of it does not teach us that at all. In fact, nature makes it impossible for some women to have long, flowing hair. Black African women wear elaborate braided and twisted hairdos close to their heads because their curly hair does not fall long naturally, So "nature" here cannot mean what we think of as nature, but rather custom — what was universally considered appropriate, attractive, and respectable in Corinth. It would seem "natural" to them.

There are several reasons why women without head coverings were disgraceful to the Corinthians. First, the Greek married woman without her head covering was labeled an adulteress. Wives were expected to be chaste, faithful to their husbands, and to busy themselves at home with children, servants, and household business. They were given little education or personal freedom. Wives could be punished for adultery, while husbands were not. However, husbands *were* punished for the adultery of their wives. For example, Demosthenes' speech against Nearea included the following:

> If a man catches anyone in the act of adultery, he who has caught him[i.e., the husband]is not allowed to live longer with his wife in the married state. If however he does this, he is to be deprived of his honor and his civil rights; further a woman, with whom a lover has been caught, is not allowed to attend divine service. If she nevertheless enters the temple, she exposes herself to every kind of assault, short of death, without retribution.[3]

Adulteresses were also punished by having their heads shaved, according to Starr.[4]

Completely apart from the standards for wives were those for the hetaerae. These women have been called prostitutes, but that is not quite accurate. They were a part of the eroticism which was so much a part of Greek life, including religious practice. Men did not consider it wrong to be sexually intimate with women other than their wives.

The hetaerae were skilled musicians and dancers, often well-educated and admired for their wit and intelligence. As entertainers and paid companions they were a natural part of the evening life of respectable Greek men. Many pictures on vases and wine jars from early Greece show hetaerae with *short hair and without headdress of any kind.*

A third class of women was the hierodule, or temple prosti-
tute. These women were slaves, purchased and given as gifts to the
goddess Aphrodite. Her temple in Corinth was famous for its
thousand priestesses, and it brought much revenue to the city.
Having sexual relations with these women was considered an act
of worship pleasing to the goddess.

What was all right for the hetaerae or hierodule was all wrong
for the married woman in the eyes of the pagan Corinthians. A man
must be sure his child was really his — that his legal heir was really
his own son. In light of these practices and moral standards, it is
easy to see that when the Christian women in Corinth left off their
headdresses when praying or prophesying, they were appearing to
be hetaerae, hierodules, or, worse yet, adulteresses. Leaving off
the headdress was dishonorable — it dishonored a wife's head, and
it also dishonored her husband's head, the seat of his honor.

Leaving off the headdress also was disgraceful because
Jewish women had to wear head coverings. Since most churches
began with converted Jews and first met in synagogues, it was
natural for some early church practices to reflect synagogue customs. Talmudic literature of the time illustrates the Jewish attitude
toward head covering: "Why does a man go about bareheaded
while a woman goes out with her head covered? She is like one
who has done wrong and is ashamed of people: Therefore she goes
out with her head covered."[5]

At first glance, 1 Corinthians 11:8,9 seems to be making a
firm statement about woman's inferior position to man. Taken
alone, the verses certainly sound that way. But in verses 11 and 12
man and woman are shown to be equal and interdependent "in the
Lord." Is Paul in verses 8 and 9 referring to some common view
but then refuting it in verses 11 and 12? It is really not clear what
verses 8 and 9 mean in the light of verses 11 and 12. Consequently,
it is poor interpretative practice to argue for the subordinate position of women from this passage. What is clear is that in Christ
they are equal to men.

Paul may be appealing further to common reasons for the
inappropriateness of uncovered heads when he refers to "the

angels.'' Jewish apocalyptic literature of the time referred to the need for women to wear a head covering to ward off the attack of evil spirits.[6] This is not to say that Paul agreed that this was a good reason to wear the head covering, but that the common belief in this reason was further evidence that it was not considered proper to go without one.

Another reason for Paul's concern about women's head coverings at Corinth may have been his desire to counter early Gnostic influence. Gnosticism was not a formal religious belief but a philosophy which filtered into the religions of the time. It was a problem in Judaism as well as Christianity, and much of what Paul says to the Corinthians in both epistles could have been intended to discourage Gnostic practices. Gnostics reportedly had an aversion to women covering their heads.[7]

Why was it important for the men to uncover their heads while praying or prophesying? Greek men uncovered their heads while worshiping pagan gods. They bared the head in recognition of divinity. Thus a Greek Christian man covering his head while worshiping would be taken as a sign that he did not consider Christ to be God. It would be a denial of Christ's deity.[8] He would dishonor Christ. He would also dishonor his own head by praying to a god and not uncovering his head.[9]

If women went without their head covering, they brought shame to their husbands. If husbands wore a covering, they brought shame on Christ. If Christ had behaved shamefully, He would have dishonored God. Each one was a representative of his "head" to that culture, and by behaving dishonorably (in this case by the use or misuse of head coverings) he brought shame on the one he represented.

Does this interpretation harmonize with its context? If we look back to 1 Corinthians 10, we can see a progression from principle stated to principle applied, clarification, and conclusion:

Principle Stated

10:23 — You can do anything, but some things you shouldn't do because of their effect.

10:31 — Whatever you do, consider whether it glorifies God.

11:1 — Follow my example, as I follow Christ's, in that you do
        what is profitable, not whatever you are able to do.

Principle Applied

11:3-10 — Example of a misused freedom which is unprofitable
           (head coverings).

Clarification

11:11,12 — Reminder that the example is only a custom; they are
           equal and interdependent "in the Lord."

11:13-15 — Proof of the impropriety of their misuse of freedom
           (obvious customs).

Conclusion

11:16 — This is how we live it.

First Corinthians 10:32 is a part of 11:1. Paul imitates Christ
in that he seeks not his own good but the good of the many in
order that they might be saved. Paul is not advocating himself as a
perfect example to follow in everything; he is referring to his
preceding statement that Christ is the perfect example.

He commends the Christians in Corinth for remembering the
instructions he gave them, but he wants them to understand that
they should not do things against custom but to "behave in such a
way that you cause neither the Jews, nor the Greeks, nor the church
of God to stumble" (10:32 MLB).

What follows is in the same train of thought as his instructions
on meat: "Everything is allowed, but not everything is helpful"
(10:23 MLB). To go against the customs of Jews and Greeks so
radically would only cause Christians to be suspect and ridiculous
to those around them.

It was not that the Corinthians were to follow *every* custom,
but this custom of head covering was important there because of
its moral significance for women.

How can this passage possibly support the "chain of command" hierarchy, when Paul shows them the contrast between

their custom and that which is true "in the Lord" (vv. 11,12)? He rejects the *basis* of the custom, which was the inferiority of women; but he insists on the *practice* to protect their reputations. F. F. Bruce has commented:

> There is nothing frivolous about such an appeal to public conventions of seemliness. To be followers of the crucified Jesus was in itself unconventional enough, but needless breaches of convention were to be discouraged. A few decades later, if not as early as this, people were ready to believe the most scandalous rumours of what went on at Christian meetings; unnecessary breaches of customary propriety would be regarded as confirmation of such rumours. It was far better to give the lie to them by scrupulous maintenance of social decorum. Though the application of the principle may vary widely, the principle itself remains valid, especially where the public reputation of the believing community is likely to depend on such externalities.[10]

1 Corinthians 14:34,35

> Let the women keep silent in the churches; for they are not permitted to speak, but let them subject themselves, just as the Law also says. And if they desire to learn anything, let them ask their own husbands at home; for it is improper for a woman to speak in church.

This passage is used in varying degrees to bar women from active participation in the public worship services of the church. In some churches women may not take part in business meetings except to vote silently, since nominations, motions, or seconds would involve speaking. Other churches allow participation in varying degrees but still restrict women's public ministry. The passage above is often cited in conjunction with "I do not allow a woman to teach or exercise authority over a man" (1 Tim. 2:12). Actually it does not say the same thing, for in 1 Corinthians the women are told not to *ask questions;* teaching is not mentioned.

There are a number of problems with these interpretations. They are inconsistent with Paul's known practices — he did allow women to speak in the church. He has just told them in chapter 11 that when they speak they should wear their head coverings. The restrictive interpretations make no provision for a woman who does not have a believing husband of whom to ask questions at home. What is she supposed to do? And as for the law mentioned, there is nothing in the Old Testament forbidding women to speak.

There is a clue in verse 35: "It is improper for a woman to speak in church." Why was it improper? It is known that women in the synagogues were nonparticipants, yet they were not necessarily silent. In fact, there is evidence that sometimes they were noisy and loud, shouting from their segregated balcony to their husbands below to ask the husbands' opinions on points being discussed. There were rulings in the Talmud concerning women being quiet in the synagogue (Meg. 23a). So, the "Law" Paul referred to was probably the synagogue rule. It was improper behavior and there was a rule against it, but it was done anyway. He wanted to quiet the noisy, disruptive meetings of the Corinthian church.

This passage is one of several instructions to that end. He previously told the Corinthian Christians to be quiet when speaking in tongues unless there was an interpreter present, and to be quiet in prophesying when someone else was speaking. The instruction to women is in a series of exhortations to do things "properly and in an orderly manner."

It is not surprising that the women would have had this problem. Most women at that time were not well-educated, as verse 35 seems to suggest: "if they desire to learn anything." In a sense, their position may have been similar to that of children who are suddenly given the privilege of participation. They did not yet know how to handle it.

So, rather than a rule permanently sealing women's lips, this seems to be an exhortation to order referring to a particular abuse — noisy interruptions by women in worship services.

Ephesians 5:22-24

Wives, be subject to your own husbands, as to the Lord. For the husband is the head of the wife, as Christ also is the head of the church, He Himself being the Savior of the body. But as the church is subject to Christ, so also the wives ought to be to their husbands in everything.

This passage has been interpreted to mean that wives must do whatever their husbands require, regardless of its propriety or moral significance. As one woman said, "If my husband told me to lie, I would do it, and I would be innocent because it was his responsibility since he told me to do it." This is the working out of a literal application of this passage, for it *says* "in everything." And if we are to apply it literally, that is the result we are left with. If your husband tells you to murder, you murder. This extreme application is unacceptable to most Christians, so they compromise by saying that it means *everything that is not wrong to do*. This is a confusing solution, for who decides what is wrong? And how wrong does it have to be before the wife refuses? Obviously these verses are hard to deal with even on this level.

The word *head* has been used to prove divine "order of command" in which the husband takes his direction from Christ and the wife from the husband. But as in 1 Corinthians 11:3, the meaning of *head* is not that of "leader" but of "source," "respect," and "responsibility."

It is interesting, but sad, that our difficulties in interpreting this passage stem from: (1) our emphasis on a nonexistent verb rather than on two obvious adverbs; (2) an ignorance of the legal position of women in Greece at that time; and (3) our habit of isolating the two verses from their context.

Bible teachers leap at the word *submit* in verse 22 and chisel it into stone as eternal law. Yet the word *submit* is not even there in the original language. One must go back to verse 21 to understand the meaning, for in the original Greek, verse 22 reads, "wives to your own husbands. . . ." It is only a phrase finishing the sentence in verse 21, with the verb understood rather than stated, and should be read thus: "Subjecting yourselves to one another, wives to your own husbands as to the Lord." However, because most English translations begin a new sentence with only a phrase (without a verb), the casual reader would think there is no connection between the two sentences.

According to Lee Anna Starr:

The Apostle [in v. 21] is here exhorting the members of the

Ephesian church to a voluntary surrender of personal preferences, one to another. The verb *hupotassomenoi* is in the middle voice. Not compulsion, but impulsion: not external pressure, but internal prompting. Not a yielding under constraint, but with ready mind.

"Subjecting yourselves one to another." The rule as here laid down is general, binding on every member of the church, regardless of sex — men as well as women; husbands as well as wives. No room for preferential rights.

It can readily be seen that under such circumstances the verb *hupotassomenoi* would be devoid of servile import. An obligation which is mutual, a duty which is reciprocal, precludes self-assertion on the part of any. No one can arrogate to himself the right to dictate. No matter what *hupotasso* may signify elsewhere, in the case before us it can only mean Christian courtesy, a due regard for the opinions of others; a readiness to make concessions in the interest of harmony and good will.[11]

The same interpretation of the verb must apply to the second phrase in the sentence (v. 22) where it is the verb understood.

Traditionally, we have emphasized the verb as a command for wives and ignored the reason for addressing wives immediately after telling all Christians to be submissive to each other. These women were already legally subject to their husbands in everything.

Ionia was a conquered province, under the sway of Rome, and the law of *Patria Potestas* held the husband responsible for the conduct of his wife; he was amenable for her offenses. . . . Roman law made the husband the sole and absolute head of his wife. His will was her law; from his decision there was no appeal.[12]

If a wife was already subject, why say it to her at all? The answer is in "*as* to the Lord" and "*as* the church is subject to Christ, *so also* the wives ought to be to their husbands in everything." The extent of their subjection was already legally established; it was their *manner* Paul was talking about. Wives could, and undoubtedly did, use the timeless methods of the underdog to get back at those who had absolute power over them. Just as slaves used sullenness, deceit, sabotage, and wastefulness to make life miserable for their masters so wives also had their ways to deal with their husbands.

But this was not the Christian way. If the wife imitated the manner of the church in serving Christ, it would be a loving, respectful service without evil motive or hidden barb. And it would not be just sometimes, or when he might find out what she had done, but in everything.

The husband also was to work out his mutual submission to his wife by using his absolute legal power over her, not to his own advantage, but as Christ exercises His power over the church, as Savior of the body. Again, it was his manner that would turn his advantage into service and loving protection, not dictatorship or authoritarianism. The "headship" concept expressed here is one of loving service and care, not one of domination.

One of the great themes in the Book of Ephesians is unity.

> I, therefore, the prisoner of the Lord, entreat you to walk in a manner worthy of the calling with which you have been called, with all humility and gentleness, with patience, showing forbearance to one another in love, being diligent to preserve the unity of the Spirit in the bond of peace. There is one body and one Spirit, just as also you were called in one hope of your calling (Eph. 4:1-4).

This unity theme recurs repeatedly from chapter 4 through 6:9, giving many practical ways to maintain it. Again and again Paul refers them to Christ's example of living in love, working for the good of others, saving and nourishing the church, His body. In other words, Christ is not a *taking* master, but a *loving, serving* Lord. One step toward unity was mutual submission; this was also a way of lovingly caring for each other. "Therefore be imitators of God, as beloved children; and walk in love" (5:1,2).

In the section following 5:21, Paul showed the believers how to work out the problems they encountered in applying equality and mutual submission to situations where Christians were not equal socially and legally. The message of this section is: Don't exploit each other. Don't misuse your power over each other. Use Christ as your example; He never misused His power.

Wives are told not to manipulate or shame their husbands, as they would not do that to Christ. Husbands are commanded not to use their wives selfishly, ignoring their needs, for Christ would never act in that way. Children are instructed to treat their parents with respect; and fathers are told not to misuse their children or take out their frustrations on them in the name of discipline, but to teach them the way the Lord would. In the slave-master relationship, slaves are cautioned not to deceive their masters, pretending to do good work while doing damage instead. Slaves are to work for Christ; Christ will honor their honest effort and reward them fairly. On the other hand, masters are not to be harsh, continually punishing, for Christ does not treat them that way. "Finally, be strong in the Lord" (Eph. 6:10), not misusing the power one has, but using it for Christ, in His way.

No matter what our social situation, the principle is the same. We must not use the opportunities we have to lord it over those under us or sabotage those above us. Our strength is not to be worldly strength to oppress, control, and manipulate, but Christ's strength to lovingly serve each other, knowing each individual to be of equal value in His sight.

1 Timothy 2:11-15

> Let a woman learn quietly with complete submission. I do not allow a woman to teach, neither to domineer over a man; instead, she is to keep still. For Adam was first formed, then Eve. And Adam was not deceived, but the woman, since she was deceived, experienced the transgression. She will, however, be kept safe through the childbearing, if with self-control she continues in faith and love and consecration (MLB).

This passage has been the single most effective weapon to keep women from active and equal participation in the church. It has been interpreted to mean everything from "women cannot speak at all in church" to "women cannot teach adult males" to "women cannot teach their own husbands." It is cited to bar women from the pastorate and deny them access to the pulpit. All evidence that women did preach and teach in the early church is ignored in order to so apply this passage.

The order-of-creation argument is used to prove that man must forever dominate woman because of some supposed fatal flaw within her that caused her to be deceived.

This is one of the most difficult passages in the Bible to interpret. Virtually no scholar claims to understand the last part of the passage. Verse 15 seems to be incapable of adequate interpretation with the information we now have, because it is inconsistent with the rest of Scripture to say it means women are saved by bearing children. Furthermore, it is inconsistent with reality to insist that godly women do not die in childbirth, for many have.

Some interpret the passage to mean that woman is rescued from the effects of the Fall by the birth of the Child (Christ). But this interpretation is obviously a forced interpretation of the Greek text.

Many who use the earlier part of the passage as a proof-text to prove woman's unsuitability for the public ministry, and who claim they are certain as to its meaning, readily admit they do not know what the latter part of the passage means. Such snatch-and-chop proof-texting violates sound interpretive principles. One cannot justify isolating a verse or two from an obvious problem context and using the isolated portion dogmatically. We simply do not know what the *whole* is trying to say. For that reason, we can pose certain possibilities and speculate as to which seems most plausible. We cannot be dogmatic in insisting part of the passage is something we are sure about and the rest a mystery. The verses are linked together in meaning, whatever the meaning may be.

Possibilities:

1. First Timothy 2:11 may refer to women interrupting the service as they did in Corinth to carry on a discussion or argument with their husbands. Paul may be citing a commonly accepted Jewish saying, ''Adam was first created,'' to remind them that this behavior was considered disrespectful and thus unacceptable. If this is the case, then perhaps the last part of the passage is a refutation of that saying: a statement that women are exonerated from Eve's part in the Fall as a vehicle to Adam by being a vehicle for the Savior (birth of the Child). This, however, is speculation and does contain grammatical problems.

It seems unlikely that Paul is telling the women that they must never speak, for in verse 8 he tells the men in what respectful manner they are to pray and follows in verse 9 with "likewise," indicating that this refers to women's public prayers which should be done in respectable and unostentatious dress. The instruction about women learning quietly follows in the same train of thought: that this is a manner worthy of women professing godliness.

Since Paul gives instructions in 1 Corinthians 11 concerning women's respectable apparel when praying or prophesying in the church, it is reasonable to interpret this passage as instructions for respectable and respectful conduct.

2. Some have suggested that there were two kinds of services in the early church and that this passage in 1 Timothy refers to the public services where visitors would think it improper for women to speak. This would not apply to the private meetings of believers, where women had equal freedom to speak.

3. Another view is that there were different classifications of teachers in the early church and the term *teacher* was different from *prophet* or *preacher* and referred to the kind of argumentative free-for-all that occurred in the synagogue, where any man could challenge the "teacher." Those holding this view feel women were probably barred from the office of teacher because it was not acceptable to the conventions of the time and thus would be offensive. They say this is why Paul mentions the husband and "domineer." This argumentative teaching would allow women to argue with their husbands publicly — a practice as unacceptable and scandalous in that culture as being argued with by one's slave.

4. Another interpretation of this passage has been proposed by Aida Spencer.[13] She points out that the Ephesian women had a tendency toward unorthodox teaching (2 Tim. 3:5b-7). Paul's answer to this situation was that the women should be instructed. "Let the women learn," he says. For Paul's time this was quite radical. Jewish women were exempted from learning the Torah (the Law). According to the rabbis, women had debatable intellectual abilities and were destined to be homemakers anyway, so there was little purpose in educating them. Normally, women did not even participate in the synagogue service.

Spencer also gives evidence from Jewish literature that it was a sign of wisdom and superior birth to learn in silence. Thus, to learn in silence was not a limitation put on the Ephesian women, but an affirmation of their capability to learn and of their worth as individuals.

Lest anyone should suggest that women were morally unfit by creation, Paul emphasizes that Eve "became" a transgressor. Paul's statement that Adam was created first does not refer to women being in perpetual submission. Rather, by speaking next of Eve's creation, he affirms her inherent worth *from* creation.

Finally, Spencer points out that verse 12 may just as accurately be translated, *"But I am not allowing* a woman to teach or have authority over a man but to be in silence."* In other words, *at that time* Paul restrained the women of Ephesus from teaching men; the women needed instruction first, lest they be deceived by false teachers just as Eve had been by Satan.

When women, through instruction, grow beyond being easily deceived, it is wrong to continue the restriction. To generalize that all women must not teach or exercise authority because of the unique problems at Ephesus would be misuse of the passage and contrary to Paul's known practice. At about this same time Paul was commending Phoebe to the church at Rome as *diakonos* and *prostatis,* words indicative of a woman active in the church and not at all fitting the restrictions at Ephesus (see pages 101,102).

Whatever the interpretation accepted as preferable, one should be careful to recognize the problems with the passage.

The principle set forth seems to be, in accord with the context, that Christians should behave in the public meetings in a respectable manner in accordance with generally accepted standards of propriety. Or, if the fourth interpretive possibility is preferred, that Christians not be allowed to teach or lead others until they themselves are grounded in the faith.

Titus 2:3-5

Older women likewise are to be reverent in their behavior, not malicious gossips, nor enslaved to much wine, teaching what is good, that they may encourage the young women to love their husbands, to love their children, to be sensible, pure, workers at home, kind, being subject to their own husbands, that the word of God may not be dishonored.

Though this passage is addressed to older women, it has been applied to young women most often. It has been taken as proof that the best, perhaps the only, vocation for women is that of wife, mother, and housekeeper. It is also a proof-text for the chain-of-command theory. Some use it to support the need for total obedience to husbands — that a woman must take orders from her husband regardless of her own inclinations, abilities, or leading from God.

The word *submit* has incorrectly been translated "obedient" in the King James Version. It is *hupotasso,* which means "to place one's self under" or "arrange oneself under." It does not imply slavish obedience. It is the same word used in Ephesians 5:21 referring to mutual subjection. Note also that women are always told to subject *themselves.* The men are never told to subject the women. It is a mutual subjection to each other, not a forced rule.

Again, this passage voices concern about Christian deportment, "that the word of God may not be dishonored."

Modern believers have incorrectly assumed that the virtues listed in this passage were particularly Christian and that pagans of the time had lower standards for wives. That is not the case. The whole point is that Christian women should make sure they came up to the moral standards of those around them. For it was not just their personal reputations that would suffer if they did not, but the reputation of their faith as well.

This early Roman epitaph illustrates the virtues praised in wives then:

> She was an incomparable wife, a good mother, a venerable grandmother, chaste, pious, industrious, honest, vigorous, watchful, careful, the true wife of one man alone, a family mother of diligence and dependability.[14]

Looking at the passage as a whole and in its context, we see Paul urging Christians to remember that liberty is not license. Christians should do what is right, because what they do is inescapably linked with Christianity in the minds of their pagan neighbors.

Neighbors would say, "She is a Christian, but see how she drinks, just like the worst old woman in the city. She is a Christian, but see how she loves gossip, even if it is harmful or untrue. She is a Christian, but see how she shames her husband, wasting his provision, and humiliating him in front of the neighbors. If that is Christianity, who needs it?"

Rather than specific commands, as part of the verse is usually interpreted, aren't these general principles for respectable and responsible living by Christian women in their respective societies?

How can we take these principles and apply them to our culture? We might say, "The women senior citizens should be good examples to the younger women, not gossips and talebearers, not character assassination specialists, not given to alcoholism, but teachers of worthwhile things, that they may teach the younger women to be sensible, thinking, responsible persons, respecting the needs of their children and husbands for love and self-esteem, to be morally blameless, keeping the priority of their families' well-being foremost, that those who hear God's Word will be reminded of a positive image and not a shameful one."

If we wanted to take these principles into another culture, we might state the admonitions differently, but the purpose would be the same — to live so that those in the culture would not automatically discount our faith because of our poor example.

In some cultures obedience to husbands would be an area where we would be tightly bound; in others it would not. We need to remember the principles the passage is trying to teach and apply them accordingly, not try to extract specific commandments.

1 Peter 3:1-6

> In a similar way you wives should be submissive to your own husbands, so that if any of them will not be persuaded by the message, they may without message be won over by the conduct of their wives, as they observe your chaste and respectful behavior.

Your adornment should not be outward — braided hair, putting on gold trinkets, or putting on robes; instead it should be the inner personality of the heart with the imperishable qualities of a gentle and quiet spirit, something of surpassing value in God's sight. For in this way the holy women of the past, who fixed their hope on God, adorned themselves, submissive as they were to their own husbands. Sarah, for instance, obeyed Abraham, whom she called "Master." You have become her daughters if you do right and are not terrorized by any fear (MLB).

This passage has been used as a proof-text to guarantee wives of non-Christian husbands that their husbands would be converted if they followed these instructions to the letter. Women have also been taught on the basis of these verses to obey their husbands as "lord and master," regardless of the command. The passage has also been used to forbid various hair styles, the wearing of jewelry, and any but the plainest clothing.

There are several factors involved in the interpretation of this passage. First, we need to understand the social situation of those who received the letter. The greeting in chapter 1 is to "the exiles of the Dispersion in Pontus, Galatia, Cappadocia, Asia, and Bithynia." This indicates Jewish Christians outside Palestine, in a Greek province with Greek customs but under Roman government with Roman laws. From several statements in the letter we understand that these people were undergoing searing persecution. They were frightened and losing hope, wondering if their faith could stand.

Why were they being persecuted? It is difficult for us as Christians to look at Christianity through the eyes of pagans in the first century. Pagans saw Christians and their strange (to them) practices as threats to their way of life, to law and order, to Roman government, and to morality. Pagan religions required moral standards and obligations that were in accord with the customs of the time. The social structure was clear-cut; everyone knew where he belonged. It was understood that some people were of more value than others. The economy was dependent upon the labor of slaves, who were generally not considered to be of much value apart from their work potential.

Along came Christianity proclaiming that in Christ everyone was equal, even slaves and masters. Preposterous! Treating slaves as equals was not only repugnant, but dangerous.

Not only did Christian liberty and equality frighten the guardians of the social structure, but it sounded a little too much like a possible early effort to overthrow Roman government. Maybe an uprising was brewing!

Then the moral problem. Those Christians were always talking about love. They said they were all one family, that they loved each other. They even had "love feasts" where everybody ate together, slave and free. Pagans misinterpreted the love Christians had for each other, flowing out of Christ's love for them. To a suspicious pagan, this sounded like immorality.

We know from 1 Corinthians that there were believers who *did* misuse their freedom and love, using it as an excuse for immorality that was shocking even to the pagan Corinthian population (1 Cor. 5:1,2). There were various rumors about Christians suggesting that they were immoral, seditious, and dangerous. Most of these rumors were based on misunderstanding, fear, or hate, but some on actual misdeeds of Christians.

The persecution against those receiving Peter's letter was especially strong. Much of the letter is spent telling them how to avoid as much trouble as possible by adhering strictly to the laws and moral codes where they found themselves, whenever such regulations did not conflict with Christian conscience. In 1 Peter 2:11,12, Peter begins a section of specific instruction to this end: "I implore you, dear friends, as aliens and exiles to keep from gratifying fleshly desires such as war against the soul. Conduct yourselves well among the Gentiles so that, although they may defame you as criminals, they may see your good works and glorify God in the day of visitation" (MLB).

All Christians are to obey the laws and officers of the law (2:13-17). Slaves are to obey their masters and give good service (2:18-25). Peter also counsels wives on dealing with unbelieving husbands (3:1-8) and husbands on dealing with unbelieving wives (3:7). His conclusion is that Christians must do good even in response to evil, for it is better to suffer for doing right than for doing wrong (3:8-17).

Roman law placed women under the complete control of their husbands. Thus, Christian wives were in a position to be easily persecuted and mistreated by unbelieving husbands. A woman might greatly desire to see her husband converted but have little power to influence him in religious matters. Peter says, in effect, "Actions speak louder than words."

The reference to fancy hairdos, jewelry, and clothing was particularly important to women wanting to be taken seriously about their faith. Upper-class Roman women were the fashion pacesetters for the whole empire, and their excesses were well-known.[15] The Roman matron spent most of her time having her hair dressed by her own personal *ornatrix,* going to the public bath, and then getting fancied up again. Bright silk robes and lots of trinkets were the rage. Their chief desire was to look elaborately stylish. But they had little depth. Aside from adorning themselves, gossip was their favorite pastime.

The provincial woman who wanted to impress would tend to copy the Roman women. But Peter warned against this. Women were told to clothe themselves instead with a gentle and quiet spirit. Rather than attributes of universal femininity as sometimes claimed, these are the fruits of the Spirit which all Christians are to exhibit (Gal. 5:22,23). Those women were to put off ostentation and let God's Spirit clothe them with qualities which would attract their husbands to Christ.

I can't help but compare this passage with the instructions in some manuals and courses for Christian wives, which tell women to manipulate their husbands with all sorts of wiles, maneuvering, and clothing. God says here, through Peter, that it is not to be outward tricks that change the husband, but inward qualities, Christian qualities from the Spirit, of great value in God's sight.

The reference to Sarah is unfortunately not translated accurately in most versions, so the import is lost. The word usually rendered "lord" or "master" is better translated "sir," for it was a term of respect, not servitude. Sarah treated her husband with respect and addressed him with respect.

The root meaning for the word here translated "obey" is the same as the word in Genesis 16:2 where it says Abraham "listened" or "hearkened" to Sarah, his wife. These words mean more than just listening, though. They mean, "I hear and therefore it is understood that I will comply." Listening is stated and obedience is understood.

The point is, Sarah and Abraham responded in the same way to each other. Abraham did what Sarah requested, and she did the same for him. This attitude is consistent with the instructions to husbands which follow those to wives (v. 7), for people cannot be joint heirs unless they are equals. A man could not hope to have his prayers for his wife's conversion answered if he did not treat her considerately and as a joint heir "of the grace of life."

These seem to be examples of mutual respect and mutual submission (Eph. 5:21) in marriage — one in the Abrahamic patriarchy and one in Peter's time in Greek culture. Marriage laws and customs change with time and location, as does the status of women. But the principles of mutual respect and mutual submission seem to be timeless, capable of application in any era or any culture.

As I look back at the preceding passages, I am struck with their similarity of context. They so often come in a series of instructions to wives, husbands, slaves, and masters. Over and over the instruction is linked with not giving unbelievers reason to disparage Christianity because of foolish or unseemly conduct by Christians. Contemporary illustrations are repeatedly given to prove that these actions were unconventional and subject to misinterpretation or scandal.

The great tenets of Christianity are freedom and love. In the first century A.D. the great oppressions were slavery, tyranny, fear, and hate. What an appeal Christ must have had! What new and wonderful joy the believers must have felt as they experienced the love and freedom in Christ which they had never had in the world.

Yet some of their problems grew out of these same sources. They claimed to be free, therefore their masters and political overseers suspected and feared them. Believers preached and practiced love, breaking down "proper" barriers. "Perhaps they are immoral!" was whispered about them.

So Paul and Peter patiently kept telling the Christians, "Don't give our accusers fuel for their stories. You may be free, but they do not understand. They think you want to be unlawful and immoral. *They do not understand, so live wisely.*"

Since we do not live in a parallel situation, should we disregard these passages and say they do not apply to us? No. But we should interpret them wisely and not separate them from their contexts to prove our biases or misconceptions. Nor should we ignore the rest of Scripture to make them mean something they do not. We must study these verses carefully and try to understand what God was trying to teach those Christians; we must use the principle illustrated even if the specific instruction is not transcultural. Christian principles are changeless, but the manner in which those principles are applied must change as customs change. By ignoring cultural factors, we have often denied many of those principles by insisting on a rigid, literal, transcultural application of these passages.

We drive away unbelievers even now by some of our rigid rules regarding women. Women outside Christ are saying, "We reject a God who treats half His human creation as second-class creatures." They are taking our actions as representative of God's attitude. We, by our practices in the church, cause "the word of God [to be] dishonored."

Notes

[1] For a more detailed treatment of the subject see: Bernard Ramm, *Protestant Biblical Interpretation* (Boston: Wilde, 1956).

[2] Lee Anna Starr, *The Bible Status of Woman* (Zarephath, NJ: Pillar of Fire, 1955), p. 28.

[3] Verena Zinserling, *Women in Greece and Rome* (New York: Abner Schram, 1973), p. 24.

[4]Starr, *The Bible Status of Woman*, p. 302.

[5]Gen. Ber. xvii. 8 as quoted in Rosemary Radford Ruether, *Religion and Sexism* (New York: Simon and Schuster, 1974), pp. 126,127. There are several references in the Talmud to the inappropriateness of uncovered heads for women. "A woman's hair is a sexual incitement . . ." (Ber. 24a). If a man uncovered the head of a woman it was considered an insult and he must pay four hundred *zuz* (Ket. 66a). One of the grounds for divorcing a wife without her *kethubah* (a kind of dowry) was if she went out without her head covered (Ket. 72a).

[6]Ruether, *Religion and Sexism*, p. 126.

[7]Ibid., p. 125.

[8]Starr, *The Bible Status of Woman*, p. 301.

[9]See also F. F. Bruce, *New Century Bible*, I and II Corinthians (London: Oliphants, 1971), pp. 104,105.

[10]Ibid., p. 107.

[11]Starr, *The Bible Status of Woman*, pp. 244,245.

[12]Ibid., p. 246.

[13]For detailed presentation of this interpretation see Aida Dina Besancon Spencer, "Eve at Ephesus," *Journal of the Evangelical Theological Society* (Fall 1974): 215-22.

[14]Zinserling, *Women in Greece and Rome*, p. 51.

[15]Ibid., pp. 70,71. "Great popularity in Rome, as everywhere in the Hellenistic world, was enjoyed by the *chiton* girdled high under the bosom, and the fine, closefitting Tarentine and Coan silk dresses, which with their attractiveness and bright colours first found favor among the venal serving maids of Aphrodite and then became the general fashion among elegant ladies. From Egypt and the Orient came new, costly textiles, threaded with gold and purple-dyed, of wool, cotton and silk. . . . Roman ladies loved ornamentation. Some of them festooned themselves — this was especially true of the less distinguished women — with fortunes in precious stones and gold ornaments. Pearls, emeralds, beryls and opals were much prized, while jewelry of glass, amber, and coral was preferred by the middle class. Forty million sesterces was the value of the jewelry of Lollia Paulina, one of Caligula's wives."

See also, Susan G. Bell, *Women: From the Greeks to the French Revolution* (Belmont, CA: Wadsworth Publishing Company, Inc., 1973), pp. 63-67.

6

What Can Woman Do?

6

What Can Woman Do?

And let her works praise her (Prov. 31:31).

What can women do? And is it all right with God if they do everything they are able to do?

Most people will admit that women *can* do anything men can do, but they often argue that women can't do most things as well as men or that God doesn't really want them to. Since we are looking at women biblically, what does the Bible show women doing with God's direction and approval?

Now, some will say that certainly women have done many unusual things in the Bible, but that doesn't mean that is what God *wants* women to do. They believe those women were exceptions and were only used because there weren't any men available at the time. Thus, God had to use women to get the job done. But I find nothing in the Bible about God's "permissive" will rather than His "direct" will concerning the work of women.

Another issue raised when talking about what women may and should do is the issue of being wife and mother. I often read Christian writers who say God's calling for women is to be wives and mothers, not doctors, lawyers, etc. Now, *wife* and *mother* are words referring to *relationships,* not occupations. The male counterparts are *husband* and *father*. And you never even consider the

89

possibility of someone making a statement like, "God wants men to be husbands and fathers, not bakers, laundry truck drivers, and accountants"; because everyone recognizes that a man can be a perfectly good husband and father and still drive a laundry truck. It is not doing the physical work connected with house-keeping and child care, such as washing dishes and diapers, that makes one a successful wife and mother, but the time, attention, and conscientious effort one puts into the *relationships* these words identify.

So, one could be a rich woman who never washed her own dishes, baked a cookie, or scrubbed a crib sheet and still be a fine mother because her relationship with her children and care for them are not dependent upon the menial tasks necessary for their care, but rather on the quality of her attention to them and her provision for them. Accordingly, she could send out her husband's shirts, have a live-in maid, cook, chauffeur, and work as president to a company and still be a great wife because her wifery would be dependent on her relationship with her husband. On the other hand, she could be a perfect housekeeper and a gourmet cook and still be a poor wife and mother.

Instead of saying that women should be only wives and mothers, we should say that wives and mothers should carefully maintain those extremely important relationships and give them top priority. The same is true for husbands and fathers.

The work of a home and family is another matter. It is honorable work that must be done and should not be disparaged, and each family should decide among themselves how they will divide and distribute the work. But let's not equate the terms wife and mother with job roles when we are really talking about rela-tionships.

There are passages in the Bible about women whose relation-ships as wives or mothers demanded hard things of them, and they met them with courage and strength. I believe God wants us all to do the same. However, no one is arguing about the faith of Jochabed (Exod. 2:3) or the raw courage and tenacity of Rizpah (2 Sam. 21:10-14), who stayed by the slain bodies of her sons and nephews, guarding them day and night until the rains came and King David was shamed into giving them a decent burial. But there is argument about what women should properly *do,* whether women may rightly have positions of leadership or jobs that tend to be reserved for men. Let's look at the Bible and see what women have done.

Activities of some Bible women seem even more striking when we remember they were living in a stronger patriarchy than the one in which we find ourselves. In the time of the judges a woman could be set out to feed the sexual appetites of the neighbors to protect a male visitor from homosexual assault, as in the story of the concubine who was subsequently cut in twelve pieces and sent as an object lesson to the twelve tribes. But even in times like that, God used a woman as a judge and military leader.

The women in this chapter do not constitute all the women in the Bible who did notable things. This is merely a sample to show that the Bible does not support the idea that God limits women to certain activities and does not want them to be leaders. God used women for jobs both usual and unusual in their culture and can do the same with us today. There are no immovable sex lines drawn on God's employment sheet.

JUDGES AND MILITARY WOMEN

I never hear a sermon about Deborah and Jael. This exciting and enlightening story from Judges 4 and 5 does not in any way fit the stereotypes of women that we have been taught. That may be one reason for the silence.

Deborah

Deborah was first of all a prophetess. Prophets in the Old Testament told the Israelites what God wanted them to know about Himself, warned of danger, gave instruction, and rebuked when necessary. I can only assume she did the same.

Deborah is identified as the wife of Lappidoth, just as Barak is identified as the son of Abinoam. Her husband is not mentioned again. She was not serving under the authority of her husband or any other man; she was being identified as that certain Deborah, probably because there were many women with the same name.

Deborah the prophetess was a judge at that time. That is, the Israelites came voluntarily to her and asked her to settle disputes.

As the scene opens, the Israelites had been twenty years under the oppressive rule of the Canaanite king. They had done "evil in the sight of the LORD, . . . And the Lord sold them into the hand of Jabin king of Canaan" (Judg. 4:1). They had cried out to the Lord to deliver them.

And now the Lord answered through Deborah. She sent for Barak and gave him God's command. He was to gather ten thousand men from the tribes of Naphtali and Zebulon and go to Mount Tabor. Sisera, the opposing commander, would be defeated at the brook Kishon.

Barak was willing to go, on one condition: that Deborah accompany him as commander-in-chief. Now, I have heard *this* preached on, but only as an example of cowardice in men. I'm not so sure it was cowardice at all. It is obvious from the account that Deborah was considered a wise woman, a woman of God. In later years it was customary to take the ark of the covenant out to battle to ensure the presence of the Lord with the army. Instead of cowardly action, this may have been a man who wanted to make sure he had the best advice at hand and the most authority with his troops. It would be one thing for him to round up ten thousand men alone, telling them that God wanted them to fight a superior force at the brook Kishon, but quite another for him to arrive with the recognized authority of Deborah.

Perhaps Barak thought that with Deborah beside him he could not fail to receive high honor when he defeated Sisera. But Deborah told him that the real honor would belong to a woman, not to him or any one of his soldiers.

Barak and Deborah arrived at the battle site, and Sisera soon approached with his nine hundred iron chariots — fearsome war machines — and all his allies. Here was a superior force with superior weapons coming against the conquered tribesmen. Then Deborah said, "Arise! For this is the day in which the LORD has given Sisera into your hands; behold, the LORD has gone out before you" (4:14). Then the battle began. Sisera's troops became confused and in turmoil, the battle went against them, and Sisera fled on foot to save his own life.

Jael

As the Israelites slaughtered his army, Sisera reached the tent of Jael, wife of Heber the Kenite, "for there was peace between Jabin the king of Hazor and the house of Heber the Kenite" (4:17). Sisera felt this was friendly territory because Heber was not an Israelite. But Heber was a descendant of Moses' father-in-law and not as unallied with the descendants of Moses' people as Sisera hoped.

Jael saw her opportunity and seized it with speed. She went out to meet Sisera and offered him asylum in her tent. He asked for a drink of water, but she gave him milk instead, perhaps hoping it would lull him to sleep. He did sleep. Then she, using her only weapons at hand, quietly placed a tent spike against his temple and drove it home with a hammer with all her strength so that it pierced his head and went into the ground beneath him. Jael left the tent, found Barak searching for Sisera, and told him to follow her.

So the nation of Israel was free again. The peace lasted for forty years this time. And the glory went to the Lord, and honor for the capturing of Sisera to a woman. But we never hear about it. Our daughters do not know that Deborah was a commander-in-chief, a supreme court justice, and a writer of a glorious song of victory. They do not know that Jael was a brave woman who did what she could with what she had when the moment presented itself.

What is the lesson in these two chapters of the Book of Judges? There are many, but certainly one is that God can do His work with small forces, in unlikely ways, and with whomever He pleases. And He pleases to use women.

DIPLOMATS

Mention is made of two unnamed women in the Old Testament who are identified only as "wise women." In both instances they were used as diplomats. These women fascinate me. I wonder if there were other wise women who were regularly consulted, as the judges were before there were kings in Israel. Perhaps these "wise persons" were women and men who were consulted about practical matters and gained a reputation for wisdom that reached beyond their neighborhoods or cities so that they were turned to naturally in times of difficult decision or diplomatic need.

The wise woman of Tekoa is mentioned in 2 Samuel 14:2. Abner sent for her to intercede for Absalom with his father David. She presented a hypothetical case to the king. Then she revealed herself and her real mission to persuade him to bring back the banished Absalom. Her diplomatic ability was evident throughout. She was successful in her mission and went on her way.

The other wise woman is mentioned in 2 Samuel 20:16-22. Joab, David's army commander, had been pursuing a man named Sheba, who instigated a revolt against David. The man had fled to one of the northernmost cities in Israel, Abel of Beth-maccah, probably trying to escape the country.

As Joab and his army made preparations to lay siege to the city and began to batter the wall, a wise woman from the city asked to speak with Joab personally. She called to him through a crack in the gate or by some other means, and after making sure she was indeed talking with the commander, she eloquently made her case for the preservation of the city. Joab replied that he was persuaded to leave the city intact, but he must have his prisoner. She agreed and put it succinctly, "His head will be thrown to you over the wall" (v. 21).

The woman wanted there to be no doubt in Joab's mind as to the loyalty of her city. She also did not want to open the city gates, a security measure in case some of the soldiers decided to do a little pillaging. She went to the people and spoke to them "in her wisdom." Convinced, they did what was required. Joab blew the trumpet signal to send the army away, and the city was saved.

Abigail

Another woman diplomat surfaced during the time of David. This incident took place before David became king, while he was hiding from King Saul (1 Sam. 25).

Abigail was one of those unfortunate women who find themselves married to a boorish fool. She appears to have been a woman of intelligence, hospitality, and decision. For if she had not acted with the immediacy and skill she showed in her dealings with David and his band, she and her whole household might have been killed.

The situation was tense. David had, with his volunteer followers, been evading King Saul, living in caves without proper food and shelter. They had been camped for some time near Nabal's sheepherders and were a deterrent to thieves who might have stolen from Nabal if David's men had not been there.

So David felt he was justified in sending emissaries to Nabal for a token of appreciation — all on the highest level. Nabal knew what was expected of him. From the response of both David and Abigail, we know it was not an unreasonable or unlikely request. But instead of treating David's emissaries like representatives of a chieftain, Nabal treated them rudely and sent them back empty-handed. This was a slap in David's face, who had been careful to respect Nabal's property, when he could have gotten away with pilfering.

David was furious. He, a respected man in Israel, a hero running for his life from a jealous king, was being treated like a common scoundrel! David determined to annihilate Nabal and his household in revenge.

Enter Abigail who, when she heard from her servants what had been done, immediately sensed the dangerous situation. She felt a responsibility to prevent the bloodshed, waste, and, more than that, a crime that would mark David as an outlaw from then on. She immediately gave orders for provisions that could be quickly packed and sent on ahead of her. She followed. (This was the method of Jacob, who feared the deserved wrath of his brother Esau.)

By the time she reached David and his approaching company, he had been somewhat appeased by the gifts preceding her. But he continued on his way to take care of Nabal. Abigail's speech and manner were all courtesy and diplomacy. She reasoned with David; she appealed to him; she complimented him; she humbled herself before him. David's anger cooled, and he turned back.

Nabal must have deserved his name (it meant "fool"), for evidently he had no idea that his foolish treatment of David's men would bring such swift retaliation, a fact obvious to Abigail. When Nabal heard of the narrowly averted disaster, he collapsed without recovery.

Later, when David learned of Nabal's death, he sent messengers to ask Abigail to be his wife, and she said yes. I would like to think David had fallen in love with her and she with him, and that he truly valued her intelligence.

Esther

Esther was a beautiful and charming woman who was more than beautiful and charming. She was also a person of courage and diplomatic ability, who risked her life to save her people.

Esther found herself in an extremely difficult situation. Through the deceptive efforts of Haman, the king's chief advisor, all the Jews in the kingdom were to be massacred. Esther's nationality was not known in the palace, and she did not dare approach the king about the matter. For custom decreed that anyone who approached the inner court of the king without a summons was to be executed, unless the king held out his golden scepter. And Esther had not been summoned for many days.

Finally, persuaded that she was the only person who could possibly help her people, she determined to try. She and her maids and the Jews of Susa fasted for three days. Then, dressed in all her royal splendor, she approached the king. He accepted her and asked what she would like.

Esther's plan was set in motion. Her request was that the king come to a banquet and bring Haman with him. Now, the king wasn't stupid; he knew Esther had not risked her life to invite him to dinner. He knew she was just being respectfully diplomatic. So he went along to the feast. During the meal, he asked again what Esther wanted. Again she said, if it pleased the king, she would like him and Haman to come again tomorrow to another banquet, and then she would ask her petition.

On the second day the king again asked what she wanted. She

had set the scene, gone through all the proper, respectful ceremonies, and now she must make her plea.

She asked for her life and the lives of her people, "for we have been sold, I and my people, to be destroyed, to be killed and to be annihilated" (Esth. 7:4). The king was astounded. Who would contemplate such a thing? Esther pointed to her other guest, "A foe and an enemy, is this wicked Haman!" (v. 6). The king became furious. Haman was desperate and made personal appeal to Esther. This made the king even more angry. The tide was turned. Haman was hanged and his property given to Esther. Esther's adoptive father, Mordecai, was made chief advisor in Haman's place. The king gave Esther and Mordecai permission to write a document and seal it with his ring that would help the Jews reverse the effects of the intended massacre.

The Jews, instead of facing sure death on the appointed day, turned it into a day of victory over their enemies. Esther then sent out a mandate appointing the day of victory an annual holiday to be observed by Jews throughout the kingdom.

God used Esther, her personality, ability, and courage, to save His people from destruction.

PROPHETESSES

Deborah was a prophetess, but she is not the only prophetess mentioned in the Bible. In 2 Kings 22 you can read about another Old Testament prophetess whose name was Huldah.

Huldah (2 Kings 22:14-20)

Good King Hezekiah's wayward son Manasseh had plunged Israel into multiple idolatries, reveling in evil and killing many innocent people. Manasseh's son Amon continued his father's excesses and pagan worship. He was murdered by his own servants. After such a reign of terror and wickedness, an eight-year-old child was made king. Josiah, like his great-grandfather Hezekiah, became a just and good king who abhorred idolatry. But after so many years of pagan worship the people did not know how to serve the true God.

During repair of the temple, the book of the Law was discovered and brought to King Josiah. No one knew what to think of it. When they read the Law, their sins and neglect were made overwhelmingly clear to them. Was there hope for the nation, or had they gone too far into sin for God to accept them back? Josiah sent his scribe, high priest, and close advisors to find out. They went to Huldah the prophetess.

She told them all the Lord had spoken to her. On the basis of her message, Josiah set about stamping out all traces of the idolatry that had preceded him. He hoped somehow to reverse the downward path toward destruction that his wayward people had begun.

Huldah was a contemporary of Jeremiah and Zephaniah, so obviously she was not consulted simply because there were no male prophets in the land. Her gender seems to have had nothing to do with her message, her reputation, or her service to God. She was God's prophet, who just happened to be female.

Anna (Luke 2:36-38)

In the temple at Jerusalem an old woman approached a young couple who were there to dedicate their newborn son to the Lord. This old woman was Anna the prophetess, who spent all her time in the temple, fasting and making intercession, both day and night.

She recognized the child as Messiah and thanked God for Him. Yes, she said, He was the one they had waited for as the redemption of Israel.

Earlier, the devout Simeon had told Mary and Joseph essentially the same message. Then Anna confirmed it! This child, Jesus, was the Promised One, the hope of Israel.

Christian prophetesses

On the day of Pentecost, Peter stood up and quoted the prophet Joel:

> "And it shall be in the last days," God says, "That I will pour forth of My Spirit upon all mankind; . . . Even upon My bondslaves, both men and women, I will in those days pour forth of My Spirit and they shall prophesy" (Acts 2:17,18).

Here is some evidence of Christian prophetesses.

> And on the next day we departed and came to Caesarea; and entering the house of Philip the evangelist, who was one of the seven, we stayed with him. Now this man had four virgin daughters who were prophetesses (Acts 21:8,9).

> But every woman who has her head uncovered while praying or prophesying, disgraces her head; for she is one and the same with her whose head is shaved (1 Cor. 11:5).

First-century Christian women *did* prophesy. It was the crowning gift, one to be desired.

> Pursue love, yet desire earnestly spiritual gifts, but especially that you may prophesy. For one who speaks in a tongue does not speak to men, but to God; for no one understands, but in his spirit he speaks mysteries. But one who prophesies speaks to men for edification and exhortation and consolation. One who speaks in a tongue edifies himself; but one who prophesies edifies the church. Now I wish that you all spoke in tongues, but even more that you would prophesy; and greater is one who prophesies than one who speaks in tongues, unless he interprets, so that the church may receive edifying (1 Cor. 14:1-5).

The gift of prophesy is listed along with other spiritual gifts in 1 Corinthians 12:7-11, gifts distributed among believers as the Holy Spirit pleases, without sexual restriction.

Contributors to the Bible

There are speculations that two of the books in our Bible were written by women. Some feel Esther herself may have written the book that bears her name. The authorship of the Book of Hebrews has always been an intriguing puzzle. Why is there no signature on one of the most important books in the New Testament? Whose style of writing does it resemble? Scholars have looked in the book for clues. And many possibilities have been suggested, among them the co-worker of Paul, Priscilla. Many have discounted the possibility that Priscilla wrote Hebrews on the grounds that she was a woman and would not have been given such a responsible position. Others argue that it is precisely because she was a woman that her name was removed from the book early in the Christian Era, when women began to be repressed in the church. It is an interesting possibility, and some have presented a carefully reasoned case for Priscilla's authorship.[1]

There are several passages in the Bible that we know came from women. Many of the contributions women have made are in the form of songs of praise. Deborah's song of victory in Judges is undoubtedly written by her, for in it she says, "The peasantry ceased, they ceased in Israel, until I, Deborah, arose, until I arose, a mother in Israel" (Judg. 5:7).

The Magnificat of Mary in Luke 1:46-55 is perhaps the most famous outpouring of praise to God in the Bible.

Huldah's prophecy is quoted in both 2 Kings 22:15-20 and 2 Chronicles 34:23-28.

The longest passage of teaching material that we are sure is from a woman is in Proverbs 31. This chapter is well-known for its description of the virtuous woman. We forget that it all came from the lips of a woman. In verse 1 it says, "The words of King Lemuel, the oracle which his mother taught him."

Bible teachers

Priscilla is mentioned in Acts 18:2; Romans 16:3; 1 Corinthians 16:19; and 2 Timothy 4:19. Acts 18:24-26 gives an indication of Priscilla's ability:

> Now a certain Jew named Apollos, an Alexandrian by birth, an eloquent man, came to Ephesus; and he was mighty in the Scriptures. This man had been instructed in the way of the Lord; and being fervent in spirit, he was speaking and teaching accurately the things concerning Jesus, being acquainted only with the baptism of John; and he began to speak out boldly in the synagogue. But when Priscilla and Aquila heard him, they took him aside and explained to him the way of God more accurately.

Priscilla's name is mentioned before that of her husband Aquila, probably an indication of her superior ability or prominence in this matter, for it was the custom to place a woman's name after her husband's. Word order in Greek sentences often indicated emphasis, with the more important point or name coming first.

Priscilla and Aquila worked with Paul in the tentmaking trade as well as in the spread of the gospel. A church met in their home in Ephesus.

Other women are greeted in Paul's letters in a manner that seems to indicate that they were his co-workers or had a teaching ministry. Tryphena and Tryphosa are called Christian workers; Persis is called an unwearied worker in the Lord (Rom. 16:12).

CHURCH LEADERS

Phoebe's work has been obscured by poor translation. The King James Version of Romans 16:1,2, says:

> I commend unto you Phebe our sister, which is a servant of the church, which is at Cenchrea: That ye receive her in the Lord, as becometh saints, and that ye assist her in whatsoever business she hath need of you: for she hath been a succourer of many, and of myself also.

Today's English Version, the Living Bible, New American Standard Bible, and New International Version all give similar readings, calling Phoebe a "servant" and "helper."

The word rendered "servant" is the Greek word *diakonos;* it appears twenty times in Paul's letters. In sixteen of those instances it is translated "minister," in three "deacon." Only in the case of Phoebe is it translated "servant." The word should be "minister" here too. We do not know in what manner Phoebe ministered, whether in teaching, overseeing, or other practical ministries; but she was definitely a minister, not a servant. The Greek word generally translated "servant" is the word *doulos,* which referred to slaves. In this case it is definitely not accurate to use it.

In the second verse Phoebe is called a "succourer" or "helper." Again, this does not adequately reveal the true nature of her work. According to the *Wycliffe Bible Encyclopedia,*

> The Greek word *prostatis* means "patroness," "protectress," suggesting she was a wealthy woman who looked after the needs of less fortunate persons. In Athens the masculine term designated the office of a man who represented people without civic rights. Under Roman law such a patron could represent foreigners.[2]

This word *prostatis* occurs only once in the New Testament, so we have no other biblical usage with which to compare it. From classical Greek writings on through patristic writings it is used in its masculine form as chief, the leader of a party, one who stands before and protects, champion, defender, ruler, leader, supporter. The word is rare in its feminine form for obvious reasons: women did not often hold positions of power in Greek culture. *Thayers Greek Lexicon* gives the primary meaning for this word as "a woman set over others."

Phoebe may well have been a leader in the church at Cenchrea and may have carried Paul's letter to the Romans to its destination.

Euodia and Syntyche

Euodia and Syntyche are often presented as examples of petty squabblers. But I do not think that does justice to those two women.

> I urge Euodia and I urge Syntyche to live in harmony in the Lord. Indeed, true comrade, I ask you also to help these women who have shared my struggle in the cause of the gospel, together with Clement also, and the rest of my fellow-workers, whose names are in the book of life (Phil. 4:2,3).

These women were leaders in the church at Philippi. Previously co-workers with Paul, they now seemed to be in danger of dividing the Philippian congregation over some issue. Paul's direct and loving appeal to them by name indicated his confidence that they were responsible women who would recognize the importance of their influence and work to reconcile their differences.

Junia

Junia was possibly another woman leader in the early church. Romans 16:7 sends greetings to "Junia . . . of note among the apostles" (KJV). Other versions give the name as "Junias," probably reflecting the translators' opinion that the person was male. However, the grammatical form of the name in the Greek text is more likely a variation of "Junia," a common name for women. "Of note among the apostles" may mean that she held the apostolic office as Paul did or, in a wider sense, that she was a "messenger" (a "sent one"). Or, the phrase could mean that she was well-known among the apostles, whichever meaning "apostle" has here. In any case, the phrase indicates that Junia was a person of influence in the church.

BUSINESSWOMEN

Christian women are often told that the world of business is outside their "sphere" and inconsistent with their "role" in life as wife and mother. However, it was not unusual for women to manage businesses in the past, and there are some interesting businesswomen in the Bible.

Lydia, the first convert in Asia, was a seller of purple. This could either mean she sold the popular dye made from a certain sea mollusk or that she sold fabric in this color. Some have assumed she was a well-to-do merchant with a business establishment. But she was almost certainly not so high on the social ladder. In Greece the merchant class was among the lower classes of society. Business was conducted from stalls in the marketplace. Lydia was a working woman; she sold purple for a living. She had a household to support, and at least some of them probably worked with her.

Priscilla was a tentmaker. She, her husband Aquila, and the apostle Paul all earned their livings at that trade.

In Proverbs 31:10-31 we find a remarkable woman. Not the "Total Woman," or the "Fascinating Woman," or the "Fulfilled Woman," or any other kind of lopsided woman, but the *virtuous* woman — God's woman. And she is amazing! She manages a household of servants. She is a farmer, a careful buyer of land and property, and a manufacturer. Even her husband is known and given a place of honor in the city because of her. Quite a businesswoman.

What *can* a woman do? And is God glad if she does it? I conclude that a woman can do anything — provided God is the One directing her to do it. Women are God's persons, who just happen to be female. Sometimes that matters, and there are special jobs that only women can do, as in the cases of Esther or Mary. And sometimes it doesn't matter at all. But femaleness does not put women in some special category that exempts them from the mainstream of God's message or His provision for service.

God entrusted women with some of His most important tasks. He sent women with the resurrection news to the rest of the disciples. Jesus accepted women into full discipleship. He commended Mary of Bethany for her efforts to sit at His feet and learn, rather than do the accepted thing and retire to the kitchen.

To those who say women cannot fill positions of leadership, the Bible says, women did. As the great evangelist D. L. Moody replied when someone asked him what a woman can do to serve Christ, "What could they not do?"

Notes

[1] Ruth Hoppin, *Priscilla: Author of the Epistle to the Hebrews* (New York: Exposition Press, 1969); Lee Anna Starr, *The Bible Status of Woman* (Zarepath, NJ: Pillar of Fire, 1955), pp. 188-206.

[2] Charles F. Pfeiffer, Howard F. Vos, and John Rea, eds., *Wycliffe Bible Encyclopedia* (Chicago: Moody Press, 1975), vol. 2, p. 1328.

7

What Do I Do Now?

7

What Do I Do Now?

I need a place where I can bring all of me to talk with people who are responding from all that they are. That seldom happens between people who are responding out of roles, theological positions or psychological models. It does happen when one authentically human person touches another.[1]

We may choose to say there are pre-ordained roles for men and for women. We may live in such myth and have that certain security. But the evidence is against it. We may deny the responsibility which we have for the definition of our roles and behavior, but if we deny the responsibility — that we have made our roles, then we have given up our power to change our roles.[2]

Suppose we are all equals before God and He shows no partiality. Suppose He really is an Equal Opportunity Employer. Where does that leave you? Here you are, a housewife with four children — do you get a baby-sitter and trudge off to seminary? Suppose you have a job you like, but it isn't anything exciting, just a job. Must you become an activist at work and turn the place upside-down so you can have equal rights? If you are convinced that God sees you as having all the qualifications to do a job your husband is convinced only men should do, do you argue him into the ground, just do what you think is right, or leave him?

It is much easier to lay forth proofs of equality in essence than it is to tell people how to change their individual lives to attain that equality in practice. I think the most important thing to remember is that the Lord did not make changes that left victims. He laid a foundation that would eventually make the subjugation of any class of people obnoxious to Christians. But He did not rip up families to do it. Nor did He ruin the finances of persons owning slaves by suddenly having them all freed. He worked with people as individuals and changed their hearts, and then their lives. Changes would come as a result of those changed hearts and lives; but if they were Spirit-directed changes they would heal, not wound — mend, not destroy. They would be wise changes.

We must begin *where we are* and be God's person there. We must look around us in our closest surroundings and say, "What do You want me to do here, Lord?" And *nothing* we do toward freeing ourselves should be done without His guidance. Good principles, without the Holy Spirit's direction, evolve into bad rules. We must remember Christ's manner and be imitators of Him as dearly loved children; and whatever is done should be done with His direction and help. This will mean that some changes may be slight and slow in coming, but others may be breathtaking as we make ourselves available for God's use for whatever He tells us to do.

Many Christian women are uncertain about what their relationship to the feminist movement should be.[3] They see worthwhile efforts they would like to be a part of, yet they are troubled and repelled by radical feminism and such emphases as abortion on demand. They wonder if they can be a part of the movement and still be true to their consciences and to Christ.

Part of the problem is that feminism does not consist of one group but several. The movement can be loosely divided into two wings — the moderate and the radical. The news media do not differentiate between groups when reporting on the activities of feminists; so it appears, on the surface, that the extreme statements and purposes of the radicals are representative of all feminists. This is not so. It is true that all feminists have a common goal of helping woman to take her place along with man as an equal human being. But from there the camps divide. Radicals, an outgrowth of the student movements of the sixties, would go on and change society drastically. They see the nuclear family, marriage, and capitalism as enemies of women and would modify them severely or do away with them altogether. On the other side of feminism are the moderates who want to work through legal and peaceable channels to give women equal opportunities in education, jobs, and under the law.

The Christian woman who chooses to work for equal opportunities for women need not fear that she is automatically aligning herself with a group of wild, extremist, anti-everything women. She can work either within an organization she can comfortably be a part of or as an individual.[4]

Those who downgrade feminism often do not realize that it had Christian beginnings and is responsible for the voting privileges women now have. The early feminists in America were Christian women who were working for the abolition of slavery. They began to realize that slaves were not the only people without human rights. They enlarged their goals to include equal rights for women as well as black people. Eventually they channeled all their efforts toward getting the vote, even though it was only one of their goals. It took so long to attain the vote that many of the founding women did not live to see it accomplished, though they had spent the major part of their lives working for it. After suffrage was secured, the feminist movement gradually disbanded without going on to work for the rest of the early feminist objectives. It seemed that the movement was dead until it erupted again in the sixties with the publication of Betty Freidan's book, *The Feminine Mystique.* It became a rallying point where women began to organize again to finish the work of the first feminists.

But should we take part in efforts to change social inequities? Many Christians have an isolationist philosophy that keeps them from participation in social reform. They feel the world is so hopelessly corrupt that the only thing they should do is work in their local churches and wait for the Rapture.

We are told to be salt and light in this world. And we cannot do that if we isolate ourselves from the needs of the world. The Lord healed the sick and fed the hungry, and not just to get them to listen to a sermon.

Christians complain about corruption in government, yet few will run for political office. They complain about the deteriorating public school system, yet few try for school board positions. If we only complain and denounce the evils and inequities around us, we are not being salt and light; we have no positive impact at all.

> Therefore to him that knoweth to do good, and doeth it not, to him it is sin (James 4:17 KJV).

> As we have therefore opportunity, let us do good unto all men, especially unto them who are of the household of faith (Gal. 6:10 KJV).

I don't think we can just turn off the world and ignore its needs. And we certainly should not ignore injustices or abuses within the church itself. I think as Christians we must do what we can — again, with God's leading and His help.

What do we do when those who are supposed to know more about the Bible than we do tell us we are making a big mistake in insisting on reading that Book for ourselves and doing what God leads us to do even if it goes against their ideas of our "place"? What do we do when we are "put down"? We can give answers to those who really want to know, if we have those answers. If we do not have the answers they want, then we should admit it and tell them the truth — that we are living by the light we have.

We are under no obligation to answer those who only want to toy with us or make fun of our desires and actions. Make no mistake, there will be put-downs and anger and even cruelty for many who quietly go about doing what they think is right for them. When we cross prejudices, we ignite violent emotions in some people. We must be gentle, but firm, and prepared for opposition. We do not need to be harsh and cutting or return sarcasm for sarcasm. Courage and conviction are much better weapons for both defense and offense.

Do not be afraid of "experts." There are no experts who

know everything. Even they can be wrong. Those who expound on the biblical teachings concerning women generally base their comments on the comments of those who preceded them so that opinion is passed down little changed or examined. We need more study in this area. In my research for this book I found a great lack of knowledge on the part of Bible scholars in the area of customs concerning women. Many seemed to know little or nothing about Greek and Roman women during the time the New Testament was written. They were ignorant of the customs affecting women's lives as reflected in secular writings of the time. The commentators usually confined themselves to quoting other commentators and a few early Christian writings.

I hope some of those bright young women in our Bible colleges and seminaries will use the minds God has given them to contribute to the knowledge we need. I hope they will persevere and learn all they can and then use it for everyone's benefit. We need the woman's perspective in Bible interpretation.

But I do not intend to exclude men from this encouragement. I know some fine Christian men who are ready to allow their sisters into equal partnership in the church. I appreciate them more than I can express. I know they will speak for women's equality. We need more like them. It is to the credit of a man to encourage women to be strong. Only weak men demand weak women.

Remember, God does not require that we be accepted or admired for what we do, nor are we required to be successful by anyone else's standards. It is only required of stewards that they be found faithful. That is our task — to be faithful to do and be what God gives us as individuals. His requirement is that we not misuse or waste what we have. He will show us how and when and where to use it — if we will listen.

Remember who you are. You are a child of God. He is your director. You need no pope, bishop, synod, or council to tell you what you may believe or how you may serve Him. We are all priests and kings before God.

Remember what Christianity is. It is not an organized system of religious beliefs like Hinduism or Islam. Christianity is a relationship between two living persons — Jesus Christ and the believer. Any rule, regulation, or trapping of organized Christianity is superficial if it interferes with that relationship.

God has paid a high price for you. He desires your love and companionship. He wants you beside Him while He works. You two are partners. He made you, and all He made was good. If He accepts you, who are you to do less?

Whatever He says to you — do it!

Notes

[1] Wes Bryan, "Divorce Christian Style: a Point of View," *The Wittenburg Door,* August-September, 1974, p. 31.

[2] E. Mansell Pattison, "A Psychologist's Perspective on Woman's Role and Status," (tape) Denver Seminary Conference on Women, 1974.

[3] Alan Graebner, *After Eve* (Minneapolis: Augsburg, 1972). A short, concise, readable paperback on the history, contemporary components, and issues of feminism from a Christian historian's perspective. It comes with a study guide for group use.

[4] *Daughters of Sarah* is a bimonthly newsletter and paper for evangelical feminists. 5104 North Christiana, Chicago, Illinois 60625.